CHRONICLES
OF THE JUICE MAN

JUICY J
AND SOREN BAKER

CHRONICLES
OF THE JUICE MAN

A MEMOIR

HANOVER
SQUARE
PRESS

HANOVER
SQUARE
PRESS™

ISBN-13: 978-1-335-00528-1

Chronicles of the Juice Man

Hanover Square Press
22 Adelaide St. West, 41st Floor
Toronto, Ontario M5H 4E3, Canada
HanoverSqPress.com
BookClubbish.com

Printed in U.S.A.

This book is dedicated to my mother, Shirley Jean Houston;
Lord Infamous; Koopsta Knicca; Gangsta Boo;
Clinton "Nigga Creep" Brady; and Cardis "K-Rock" Burns.

CHRONICLES
OF THE JUICE MAN

PROLOGUE

FEBRUARY 2008
HOLMBY HILLS, CALIFORNIA
4:35 A.M.

I WAS HIGH AS a muthafucka. As I was stumbling through this party, I looked around. People were fucking over there. Cocaine was over here.

But this coke was different. A waiter-looking guy wearing a vest and with his hair slicked back came up to me with a wood-grain box. He opened it. "You want some?" he said as if he was offering me drink.

I looked in the box and I saw blue, yellow, cherry, watermelon, and cotton candy–flavored cocaine. I'd never seen anything like that. I was blown away.

No matter where I looked, it seemed like people were snorting all kinds of stuff. It also seemed like velvet was everywhere.

I declined the coke and walked into a bedroom. Girls were in the bed, just waiting—maybe for me, maybe someone else. I had no idea.

As I looked around the room, I noticed people were standing in a line in front of this huge closet. As I walked that way, I saw that there was a bar *inside the closet*. I was looking at the guy behind the bar.

"Hey, man," he said, ready to please. "What do you want to drink?"

"You're serving drinks?" I responded in disbelief.

This guy was serving mixed drinks *out of the closet*. That's how huge this house was. It happened to be across the street from where Michael Jackson would die about a year later.

I just walked away, making my way to the bathroom. Someone was snorting coke in there. I looked back at the bed with the girls in it. Someone was now snorting coke there, too. It was some all-out Hollywood shit.

In an attempt to gather myself, I stumbled to the balcony. I was dizzy and trying to hold on to the cup I had in my hand while I made sense of things.

For the better part of two years, I had been living in the aftermath of Three 6 Mafia's Oscar win. Everything was coming so fast. We were the first group to perform at the Playboy Mansion. Orgies became a normal thing.

I had a doctor who would get me anything. Lean. Vicodin. But my love? Xanax. I loved to take Xanax and drink. I knew you weren't supposed to do that because it can slow your heart down too much, but I didn't care. It made me feel good and that's all that mattered to me.

Since the Oscar victory, Three 6 Mafia had been on top of the world. Life had become one big party. Today's festivities happened to be at this house in Holmby Hills. Britney Spears had been walking in when I was walking out, but I'd been at the party for a few hours before I found myself standing on the balcony. Then it hit me: What am I doing with my life?

I was doing the same thing every day, just waking up and getting high. That was it. Everything was suffering. The music Three 6 Mafia was making wasn't sounding good. Our name wasn't hot anymore. That was like death to me. I loved making music. I didn't like it—I *loved* it, but it was all slipping away, one party at a time.

I felt like I'd lost all of my musical talent, that my career was over. For the first time in my life, I felt out of the loop. I was rapping about drugs, but I wasn't rapping about being a drug dealer. I was the one *doing the drugs*. I was rapping what I heard other people talking about. But I wasn't used to riding the wave. I was used to creating the wave. I wasn't even myself anymore. Right there, I knew I was lost.

I gathered myself and called the girl I was seeing at the time.

"I'm done with this shit," I told her. "I need you to come pick me up before I kill myself."

"What?" she replied.

"I'm not feeling good," I told her. "This ain't me. This really ain't where I wanna end my life."

As I waited for her, I poured out my cup. It wasn't much, but I felt like it was one small step to stop my world from crumbling.

When she pulled up, I got in the car.

"I'm done," I told her.

I knew I had to leave Los Angeles. I was losing my mind and was worried what was going to happen to me if I stayed.

Right after that, I broke up with her, sold my house in LA, packed, put my Rolls-Royce on a truck, and moved back to Memphis.

CHAPTER

1

BACK AGAINST DA WALL

MEMPHIS IS AN EVIL PLACE. Throughout my childhood, it was overrun with crime and mayhem. People
walked around like zombies high on drugs. I felt like Memphis actually was Hell.

A few months before my tenth birthday, I heard about
the Shannon Street murders. On January 11, 1983, White
police officers Ray Schwill and Bobby Hester were dis-
patched to a residence on Shannon Street in North Memphis to investigate an alleged purse snatching. They arrived
at the residence of Lindberg Sanders, a Black man with
mental illness who thought he had been resurrected after
being killed by the police.

Sanders hated the cops, referred to himself as "Black
Jesus," and had 13 of his followers at his house. They were
waiting for the moon to touch the earth—in Memphis.
Everyone who wasn't a true believer in what Sanders was

preaching would perish. Sanders and his devotees were smoking weed, drinking wine, and fasting while they waited for the moon event to cleanse the world when the officers arrived.

Seven members of Sanders' cult left when the cops showed up. After an initial conversation, Schwill and Hester were lured into Sanders' house and ambushed. Schwill called for backup, was shot in the face, and played dead while Hester was taken hostage and moved into a bedroom.

When additional officers arrived on the scene, they were met with gunfire. Once police made contact with Sanders, he stated his desire to kill Hester live on a Memphis radio station. Hester was heard begging for his life as the police negotiated with Sanders.

After police haggled with Sanders for about 30 hours, a SWAT team raided the house. The cultists and police exchanged fire, killing Sanders and his remaining six followers. Police also discovered the body of Hester, who had been stabbed, beaten, and tortured for hours before dying from his injuries. Schwill lived, despite being shot in the face.

In the aftermath of the massacre, reports surfaced that six of the seven members of Sanders' cult were shot in the head execution-style, leading many activists to claim that their deaths were unjustified. Either way, after this incident the Memphis police changed their policy. They would raid a location immediately if a hostage was injured. The force also enacted de-escalation training and had policies focusing on how to deal with mentally ill suspects.

The Shannon Street murders rocked Memphis, further driving a wedge between the city's Black and White residents. Watching the events unfold on television, I was barely able to comprehend what I was seeing taking place about a mile away from my family's residence in North Memphis.

It was a nightmare incident that felt like it made things worse in my city. Crime seemed to be everywhere, and the police were regularly beating up people, especially Black men. My family wasn't immune to hardship either. We got kicked out of our apartment, and I went to stay with my maternal grandmother, Dee Etta Brady, for a bit.

While I was there, my aunt Joyce would sometimes stop by. My aunt had a crazy-ass boyfriend. They'd get into fights all the time. One day, I saw my grandmother using a knife to pry bullets out of the outside walls of the house. I asked her what she was doing. She told me Joyce's boyfriend had shot up the house.

Bullets flying was a regular occurrence at my grandmother's house. My mom would yell "Get on the floor" or "Get down" when my aunt's boyfriend was on one of his rampages. As soon as my mom would say it, I'd hear a volley of gunshots. It wasn't just him, though. There were a lot of shoot-outs between other people in my neighborhood, but the police didn't seem to care much.

During the mid-1980s, people were messed up on crack, too. Drugs and bullets are one thing. Words are another. My mother, Shirley Jean Brady, told me that her father, Walter Brady Sr., never told her that he loved her. That's bad, especially for a girl. If you never tell your son you love him, he might not give a damn. Little girls, though, want to be loved by their daddy and feel protected.

My mom didn't feel either of those things. She had five siblings: Walter, Larry, Joyce, Deborah, and Ray. The wild thing was that my grandfather had an entirely different family with another woman. They also had several kids—and they were also named Walter, Shirley, Larry, Joyce, Deborah, and Ray. I was told that my grandfather did that so he wouldn't forget their names. It's some creepy, crazy shit, but that's the environment in which my mother was raised.

When my mother was growing up, her father took her to events at Voodoo Village, a neighborhood in Southwest Memphis developed by Wash "Doc" Harris in the 1960s. Known locally as a "spiritual doctor," he wanted the area to be a center for spiritual healing. When I was growing up, Voodoo Village had a bunch of houses that were strangely shaped and painted with unusual colors like red and blue. Some people even put dolls, crosses, stars, and other objects Harris made in their yards. Even though he called them "symbols of God," Harris' creations symbolized his cult in the eyes and minds of a lot of people in Memphis. Either way, it's a scary place. My mom grew up absorbing a lot of bad energy from and because of her family.

When my mom went outside her own house, she (and my dad, Jordan Houston Jr.) had to deal with different types of trauma: segregation and racism. My parents would tell me about how they would be called "nigger" when they were growing up, and that White people would throw bottles at them and try to kidnap them so they could hang them from a tree. My parents had to ride in the back of the bus, avoid the "Whites Only" bathrooms, and be careful when traveling out of state. When Dr. Martin Luther King Jr. was killed on April 4, 1968, my mother was on the bus on her way home from LeMoyne-Owen College, scared. People were throwing rocks at the bus and burning the city down.

That was a difficult time, one I'm glad I didn't grow up in. The racist things I experienced growing up were nothing like what my parents told me they went through. We only know the stories we see on TV or read on the internet. The people of my parents' generation *lived* it. They experienced the devastation, the brutality, the hate. It left a lasting impact on my parents, disturbing their minds and traumatizing my mother in particular. My parents had a hard time trusting White folks.

The racism I dealt with growing up was very different. It was still very strong, but it was dispensed by the police and was a lot of the same brutality we still see today. I've been racially profiled countless times and I imagine that's going to keep happening as long as the police think that young Black men are always up to no good.

Memphis, however, is also a musical city. Active since 1947, 1070 WDIA is an AM radio station based there. Soon after its launch, WDIA became the first radio station programmed entirely for Blacks. After working in comedy and dance, Rufus Thomas started recording his own songs and got a job as a DJ on WDIA.

With the excitement WDIA generated, people from all over the city would try to make it as a singer. Rufus Thomas kept recording, including the single "Bear Cat," an unofficial answer record to Big Mama Thornton's "Hound Dog." Elvis Presley recorded Thomas' song "Tiger Man" and, in 1960, Rufus recorded "Cause I Love You" for Memphis-based Satellite Records, which changed its name to Stax Records a year later.

Stax is one of the most important companies in music history, but by the time I was coming up, its run with The Staple Singers, Johnnie Taylor, Otis Redding, Isaac Hayes, The Bar-Kays, The Delfonics, The Emotions, The Dramatics, and Booker T. & The M.G.'s was pretty much over.

Regardless, there was so much soul in Memphis. You

could walk down the street and see people playing guitars. Everybody knew somebody that played the piano. The city was full of musical talent. The vibe was electric.

It seemed like everywhere I went, I heard people playing Willie Hutch, Lamont Dozier, Bobby Womack, and Al Green. I'd hear people talking about the musicians they loved back in the day, like Isaac Hayes. My dad would talk about how Isaac Hayes had a gold Cadillac. My mother would tell me how she listened to Carla Thomas, the Queen of Memphis Soul and the daughter of Rufus Thomas. She loved Carla Thomas' song "Gee Whiz (Look at His Eyes)" and was proud that she was born and raised in Memphis. I was fascinated by the stories, hearing my parents and other people talk about them. Even though I wasn't around to experience what my parents were talking about, these talks planted a seed. But that's what it was. *Talk.* Other people's memories.

I grew up in North Memphis with my mom, my dad, my older brother, Patrick (later known as Project Pat), and my two younger sisters, Carol and Cheryl. Even though Pat is one year older than me, my parents named me Jordan Houston III.

I never asked my parents why Pat, their firstborn, wasn't named Jordan. When my grandmother died, I realized I didn't know how old she was. Whenever I had asked her how old she was, she'd never answer me. In my family, some things just weren't discussed and some questions weren't asked. Early on, I learned that sometimes it's best to keep your mouth shut.

My family moved a lot when I was a child, through what seemed like all of North Memphis. When we lived in Frayser, it was different because there were a few White people there. But the White people were moving out when we were moving in. The neighborhood had a sense of community, though. I remember a lady giving away toys and me getting some.

Even then, Pat and I were starting to get into trouble. We didn't have the money to get our own things, so we became thieves. We'd break into our neighbor's house and steal their Atari games. If people would leave their garage doors open, we'd go in and grab some stuff. I'd go to convenience stores and steal toys. I was a ratchet kid.

We settled in a two-bedroom apartment in the Cypress Gardens Apartments in the Hyde Park section of North Memphis. Pat and I shared a room. My sisters were in the other, while my parents slept in the living room on a pull-out couch. Pat and I had disagreements from time to time, but we never had any arguments. We always looked out for one another. He made sure I was straight and I made sure he was straight. Pat and I looked after our sisters, too, making sure they were safe. Outside our apartment, though, there were always fights, people getting beat up, shot. It felt like we were in the middle of World War III.

My mother was a librarian and a substitute teacher. My dad was a traveling minister, and he would be out of town a lot, preaching. Sometimes he'd be gone for two or three weeks, sometimes a month. He was very devout and even told me that he'd seen an angel.

When he wasn't around, there wouldn't always be food in the refrigerator. Sometimes I'd put sugar in water and freeze it into ice cubes just to chew on something. I'd be so damn hungry, but we wouldn't have any food. Fortunately, my grandmother would bring peanut butter and jelly sandwiches from down the street to our apartment.

We'd be so happy to get those sandwiches. That's just how it was, though, so I thought that being broke was normal.

One time I was riding in this raggedy-ass car with my dad. He was bringing me home from school and I was so embarrassed. I didn't want anyone to see me, so I ducked down. But it was too late. "We saw you in that piece-of-shit-ass car your family was riding in," people in the neighborhood would say to me, laughing.

It was some tough times. My parents made sure we all went to church pretty much every Sunday, though. I remember my dad coming in to wake us up. "Rise, shine, give God the glory, glory. Rise, shine, give God the glory," he'd sing to us as we woke up and hustled out of bed. We attended Pentecostal Temple Church of God in Christ at 229 South Danny Thomas Boulevard in Memphis, which is where I was baptized. It is also walking distance from Hamilton High School, where I went for summer school. Elvis Presley went there, too, but by the time I was coming up, White flight had taken place and it was an all-Black neighborhood.

My dad was a powerful preacher. He made you *feel* what he was saying. I looked up to him like he was God Himself, like he could do no wrong. He was cool, chill, and always looked nice, clean, and shaved up. He ate a healthy diet and would drink celery juice. My father had a certain amount of clout, too. One of his deacons would carry my dad's briefcase around for him. To me, that briefcase symbolized that my father was doing important business. I remember telling him that I wanted to be just like him when I grew up.

I didn't like waking up early, but one thing made going to church a little better. After church, I'd jump on the instruments, play the drums, the piano.

Beyond the music, there was an inspirational vibe in our church. I saw people get delivered and would hear great stories of salvation. They also played us movies on the church's projector. One in particular hit home. It was about a guy who went to jail for robbing people and then turned his life around. He became a minister. Right there, I saw that regardless of how you started, you could change your life for the better.

Trouble was always around the corner, though. One of the ladies who attended our church got robbed in the Church's Chicken right next door. They snatched her purse. Those types of incidents made us feel safer in church than outside.

As if going to church Sunday wasn't enough, we'd attend night services, too. When we weren't in church, we used to pray all the time. I believe in prayer, and for good reason. I used to have a real bad allergy. My eyes would often get extremely puffy. I looked like someone had hit me in my eyes, like how a boxer looks after a fight. After this had been going on for a while, my daddy put his hand over my eyes and prayed for me. By the next day, everything had cleared up. It never came back, either.

Prayer has always been a regular part of my life. Even today, when my dad calls me over the phone, we'll have prayer on Sundays.

Back in the day, when we weren't praying, I was getting into other things. One day, I was watching television and they were talking about this basketball player Len Bias. It was June 19, 1986, and I was 13. He was a star basketball player at the University of Maryland. People now say he was like LeBron before LeBron, and he'd just got drafted number two overall by the Boston Celtics before suddenly dying. On the news, they were talking about how he over-dosed on cocaine. I'm sitting there wondering, "What the fuck is cocaine? I ain't *never* doing cocaine." That stuck in my head. It's one of the reasons why I didn't do a lot of hard drugs even though I got offered cocaine so many times. I was scared. Terrified, actually. Seeing that Len Bias story on TV, it stuck in my head and stayed with me for the rest of my life. It's sad to say, but seeing that story on the news re-ally helped me out. I never did cocaine because I felt like if I did one hit, I would die. Cocaine was around us, though.

I grew up in North Memphis around so many robbers, thieves, drug dealers, rapists, pimps, all kinds of crazy nig-gas, man. People would walk up to your house, knock on your door, and blow you away once you answered. Then the shooter would run without even taking anything. It was wild.

Right around the time Len Bias died, I'd stand on the corner and see guys with jheri curls. They were just there talking shit all day. "Say, man. This is how you do it if you want to be a drug dealer," is the type of thing they'd say to me. "I'll front you the rocks. You give me the money once you sell it and I'll cut you in on the money." These guys would talk about AIDS, about how you had to wear two rubbers because it was so bad out there.

The local pimps were also quick to add their piece. "I'd never give a bitch shit," they'd say. I was drawn to their con-fidence and to what I thought was their power. I also liked that these pimps had women and that they were fast-talking and slick. Any one of them could just talk to a woman and she'd do *exactly* what he told her to. A lot of the things they said on the corner informed my early songs such as "Trust No Bitch" and "Fuck All Dem Hoes."

Artists often draw inspiration from their surroundings. Some get their inspiration from leaves, flowers. My inspiration came from the pimps, drug dealers, and robbers. I didn't have to seek them out. They were right there as soon as I walked out the front door of my family's apartment, which seemed like a different world even though it was only a few feet away.

I would just stand there on the street and listen, soaking up everything that was going on in the streets of North Memphis. I'd be around the junkies, the crackheads, the guy in my apartment complex selling crazy amounts of drugs out of his window.

There were so many needles on the ground in our neighborhood. I used to call the junkies "blood donors" because they used to share needles with the other fiends. When somebody would overdose and die from drugs, the junkies would say, "That's gotta be the good shit." That was the drug they wanted because they knew it was powerful and would deliver a quality high. The junkies weren't worried about ODing.

The first time I'd ever seen someone die was when I saw a guy get shot seven times in the chest. Another time, police were chasing a guy who allegedly raped a woman. The police were chasing him through our projects. I saw one, two, three, four, five officers chasing him with their nightsticks raised. All the officers were White. They caught the suspect in an abandoned apartment. I went in there the next day, just out of curiosity. The police had beat this guy so bad that there was blood all over the walls. It looked like a horror movie.

Real violence was all around me. Maybe that's why I was drawn to horror movies. One of my favorites was *An Amer-*

ican Werewolf in London. The film is about two American college students, Jack and David, backpacking through Britain, who are attacked by a werewolf. Jack is killed, while David is mauled and has nightmares about his dead friend and other victims of the werewolf before becoming a werewolf himself. David cannot control his animal rage and is eventually killed by the police. The movie scared the shit out of me, but I'd watch it faithfully every time I could.

That was a distraction, though. Real life was scary enough. I remember a time when Pat and I were kids and this dude pulled out his gun and was about to shoot somebody. But when he saw Pat and me, he put his gun down. He and another guy jumped in his car and drove off. That was the exception to the rule, though. When I was 13, I saw a guy get shot five times. I wouldn't say that it taught me anything. It just showed me what could happen living in North Memphis.

That was the direct opposite of what was happening in our apartment. My mom and dad didn't cuss around us. They'd only cuss if they got really, really mad, but that was rare. Because my dad was on the road a lot, we spent most of our time with our mom.

Thankfully my parents gave us a lot of good principles to live by. However, Pat and I didn't always follow them. Pat could rap, but he really wasn't interested in music early on. He didn't feel like there was any money in it. He was partly right. In the early 1980s, only a handful of rappers had made it big—Whodini and Run-D.M.C. were two of the most popular—and everyone who had broken through was from New York. The genre was seen by most as a New York phenomenon, and one with a short shelf life at that.

Plus, rap was a small community then. It was nothing like the multibillion-dollar rap business we have today.

So it wasn't a surprise that Pat and I took two different paths. He took the street route, trying to sell dope, rob people, and stuff like that. He was in the streets 24/7. At the time, I didn't want to hang around Pat. He was doing stuff that I wasn't cool with. I felt like he was going to get into some type of trouble and I didn't want any part of that.

I had other ideas, mainly music. I used to watch *Sha Na Na*, *Soul Train*, *Solid Gold*, and the dance programs they'd have on every Saturday. I was in love with those TV shows, and I'd watch them faithfully, and I'd listen to Michael Jackson, Billy Joel, Huey Lewis and The News, Pat Benatar, Elton John, Boy George, George Michael, and Duran Duran. I thought it was weird that some of the men would have lipstick on, but I thought that was some rock-and-roll shit. I didn't dress like that, but I liked the music.

I really gravitated toward Prince, though. I wanted to be like him. He was cool, had the girls, and was mysterious with his purple motorcycle. I was also getting into rap thanks to The Sugarhill Gang's "Rapper's Delight" and material from Kurtis Blow, Fat Boys, LL Cool J, and Roxanne Shanté. I'd steal music magazines from the store, tear the photos out, and put their pictures on my wall. That was our Instagram.

At first, I wanted to be a singer or play piano. But we didn't have enough money to get a piano. My grandfather, who lived in Kansas City, had a piano. When we'd visit, my cousins there would laugh at how we talked. They made fun of our accents, how we'd say "hur" not "here," "shur" not "sure." My mom made it even worse, telling us to not talk like that, to not talk Southern. We told her that that was how we talked. Her response: pronounce your words better. My mom was very insecure about how others perceived her and us. Other than when I was very young, I never really gave a fuck about what people said.

In order to escape the hassle during our visits, I'd always try to get on the piano and play. They'd be like, "Boy. Get your ass off that damn piano. You've been on that piano all day."

I'd always tell my mom, "I've got to get ready." I'd tell her I was going to be a big music producer, that I was going to have a big house, a lot of money, a couple of girlfriends.

That was my dream. My reality was much different.

When my dad was home, we'd get on the bus and go to the grocery store because we didn't have a car at the time. I used to hate that shit. I used to tell myself that I was gonna make some money, that I wasn't gonna live like that. I didn't want to be jumping on a bus, riding a bus to the grocery store, carrying those heavy-ass groceries back on the bus in the hot sun. It made me be like, "I'm finna get about my hustle because I refuse to be living like this for the rest of my life." I told myself that if I needed to work three jobs to make ends meet, I would work three jobs.

From that point on, I had a hustle mentality. I was a hustle machine. Whenever I'd get my hands on some money, I'd save it or spend it wisely.

I saw how people were addicted to things, from drugs to money. My addiction was about to kick in, too.

CHAPTER

2

MOTIVATED

I WAS ALWAYS PRACTICING on my turntables because I felt like I was going to be this big artist. That was my dream. I'd be telling my mom that I was going to be a big producer, a big rapper, but she didn't know what the hell I was talking about. After all, she was a librarian.

But I'd be in my room all the time, scratching records all day. I would listen to Grandmaster Flash, LL Cool J, DJ Tat Money, Steady B, and Big Daddy Kane. We'd have debates about who had the best scratches. I liked Eric B. & Rakim, but Eric B.'s scratches were sloppy. I loved how Public Enemy's Terminator X did the "transformer" scratch. It got the name because, in part, it sounded like the sound the characters on the *Transformers* cartoon made when they switched from one identity to the other. But Terminator X didn't scratch throughout much of Public Enemy's albums. I felt a similar way about Run-D.M.C.'s Jam Master Jay. I was particularly drawn to DJ Jazzy Jeff & The Fresh Prince, and I would try to mimic every one of Jeff's scratches.

I even got my name from Jazzy Jeff. I wanted to call myself Jazzy Jay, but a hip-hop pioneer from the Bronx already used that. So here I was, 15, and trying to think of a name. Pat and I slept on bunk beds, me on top. I looked down and I saw this Juicy Fruit gum wrapper. I jumped down, picked it up, and said, "Juicy Fruit. Juicy J. Damn. That's kind of hard." So I called myself The Notorious Juicy J. I used to spray-paint it all over the neighborhood, on all the bike trails. I'd write "DJ Juicy J Coming Soon."

I'd gotten a piece of a turntable off the street. Soon thereafter, I found somebody that had another turntable. I gave him $20 for it. My daddy had tape recorders he recorded his sermons on, so I MacGyvered them and made a mix throttle with a wire connected to my two turntables. I was using it as a fader. If I hit the wire, the music would play over the speaker, and if I took the wire away, it wouldn't. My homemade setup, made from other people's equipment, enabled me to do my best rendition of Jazzy Jeff.

My mother didn't want me to play the music loud inside the house, so I had to do everything on headphones. I'd be in the room all day scratching, trying to figure out how to mix, and studying Jazzy Jeff. He had the best scratches I'd ever heard. I would put my ear to the speaker and be mesmerized by his scratches. I was driven to master his scratches, to be able to do each one of them just like he did. In addition to Jazzy Jeff, I was listening to Cash Money & Marvelous, Steady B, a lot of the Philadelphia guys. Philly had a lot of dope-ass DJs. I was trying to mimic every scratch, day after day, week after week, month after month.

I also used to have a speaker that I would sit outside the

window. People would come by as I was mixing and check me out. I was trying to make the best of what I had.

It was rough, but I was still scraping by. One time, I had to use the metal part of a twist tie as a needle because times were so hard. It was some ratchet-ass shit, but I was determined to be a DJ, to be the best DJ in Memphis. I was just some little kid in this little apartment trying to figure things out. Eventually, I mastered scratching and tricks on turntables.

One day I told my mom, "Look, I'm talented. I know I've got the talent, but I need to know the business of the music." In addition to the comic books and books about history, Christopher Columbus, and slavery that she was getting me, I asked my mom to get me some books about the music industry. Whatever the library had about the music industry, I wanted to read it. She got me books that talked about management, publishing, engineering, royalties. I read those five or six books from top to bottom. That gave me the knowledge of the business part of the music industry.

Soulsville U.S.A.: The Story of Stax Records is one of the most important books I ever read. What I learned in there influenced and inspired a lot of the moves I would make years later.

My dream was to re-create the excitement and energy I heard my parents and others talk about when they discussed Stax Records. Besides, I wanted to have my own Memphis record label with my own artists.

Even though my mom helped me by getting me books about the music business, she didn't like the idea of me pursuing music at such a young age. In fact, both my parents didn't like what I was trying to do with music, but for different reasons. My mom was against it because it wasn't a traditional job, like a doctor or lawyer. She didn't see the future in it. My dad didn't approve of the content in rap, but he supported me and would take me to the studio against my mom's wishes.

Going to the studio presented its own issues. I saw an ad in the newspaper for a guy saying he had a studio in his house. My dad took one of my friends and me there, but he got a bad vibe and didn't trust the guy running the studio. My dad told me we could go inside, but that he would be waiting outside in our car.

When my friend and I walked in, the only thing in "the studio" was a piano. There were two older men in there, and they told us that we could practice here and that they had more equipment at another location. Even as a young teenager, I thought these guys were on some weird shit. My friend and I left immediately.

As soon as we got in the car, I told my dad that there was only a piano in there. To this day, I wonder if those guys were on some Jeffrey Dahmer shit. Who knows how that could have gone.

I didn't give up on my studio pursuits, though. My dad had a friend who sang, Tony Sherrod. The guy was always saying that he was going to be bigger than Michael Jackson. One day, my dad needed to pick up some money from one of his friends, so I went with my dad to his friend's studio. He told me to wait in the car while he went inside. After begging him to let me come see the studio and see Tony record, he agreed to let me come to the door and wait outside. As soon as my dad stepped out, I peppered him with questions. "What were you guys doing? How were they recording?"

"He had a track machine," my dad said. He told me it was a four-track machine, one where you record the beat on one track, your vocals on another track. Every answer he gave me led to more questions. "What kind of machine was it? Where can I get one of these machines?"

All this was happening right at the studio door. "Be quiet, boy," my dad told me. My mind was racing. As we walked to the car, I started thinking about a four-track machine. I'd never heard of one, but I was fixated on getting one so I could record my own songs. I knew I couldn't afford one, but at least I was starting to learn what I was going to need.

Music was in my heart. It was all I wanted to do. While I was growing up, people in Memphis really focused on music from Memphis artists. We loved N.W.A, but by the time DJ Spanish Fly, Sonny D, DJ BK, and Pretty Tony were emerging locally, Memphis was developing its own sound. They wouldn't play other artists too much.

Since I was so focused on music, I always had problems in school. I had even failed fourth grade. When I got to junior high, I tried to change. Like a lot of other kids, the adults around me were telling me that I needed to learn how to work with computers, go to college, become a lawyer. I was only thinking about that because I felt that's what you were supposed to do. But I didn't want to do that, to sit there and just read schoolbooks all day. I wanted to beat on the table and rap. My goal was to be a musician, a producer, and an executive. I wanted to be a combination of Michael Jackson, Berry Gordy, Stevie Wonder, Prince, Barry White, Isaac Hayes, and Stax Records co-owner Al Bell, all wrapped into one.

My early raps are nothing like the music I would get

famous for a few years later. I didn't cuss in my first raps. I'd even tell my friend Lorenzo "Ren" Richards, who I started rapping with, not to cuss in his raps, either. My parents didn't cuss, so I wanted Ren and me to be like them.

My dad in particular was always on my ass around this time, telling me to get myself together, be more responsible, and think about getting my own place. I wanted to do all that, which I knew would help me handle my business with my music. As an underdog, I dreamed of the day when I would make it big. It was going to be like Biz Markie's famous song "Vapors." In the Marley Marl–produced song, Biz raps about several members of his crew who were doubted and hated on, and how people changed once they became successful. I felt that. I imagined people would do the same with me once I became a superstar.

Despite all the obstacles, I wasn't playing games. I didn't write all these raps, go back and forth to all the studios, practice scratching for hours at a time, and do all the DJ tricks for nothing. I was in it to win it.

But before I could live that dream, I needed to get out of the streets that were trying to pull me under.

CHAPTER

3

ON DA BLOCK

WHEN I GOT TO high school, there were a lot of fights—a lot of gang fights. I used to try to stay to myself, but trouble is always going to come your way regardless. I wouldn't talk to half the niggas around me and they'd be like, "Aw, man, why don't you fuck with us?" I didn't do what they did, and they didn't do what I did. They were into fights and I was into music.

Like many other kids, I tried to sell some weed and rode around in stolen cars with my friends. Riding in stolen cars was risky, though, because the police would pull young Black men over for no reason. They figured we wouldn't have had the money to buy a brand-new Oldsmobile. We knew that, too, so we'd ride around for only an hour or two, play the newest music from local stars like Sonny D, hang out the window, and holler at girls. If we rode around at night, we'd listen to the live broadcast from Club No

Name, which came on at midnight and played the sets from DJ Spanish Fly and Ray Tha Jay. After we rode for a while, we'd ditch the car somewhere. It was like a real-life version of the movie *New Jersey Drive*.

I also made much bigger mistakes. In addition to the music books I had my mom get me from the library, I had her get me books about guns because I hated the kid that lived next door to us and wanted to shoot him. Unaware of my ambitions, my mom got me *A History of Firearms*.

I studied that book and tried to make my own firearm so I could shoot this dude. I took a pole from my window, put a nail in it, got gunpowder from some firecrackers, and put a rock down the pole to serve as my bullet. I took a rubber band and wrapped it around the pole, stuck a piece of paper in the small hole, and attached a lighter to my makeshift weapon in order to provide the spark. It was really some MacGyver shit.

The next time I saw the kid standing outside, he had his back turned to me and didn't see me. I pointed my "gun" at him and was trying to light the paper. I tried and tried and tried, but it wouldn't light. Then it finally lit, but it backfired and blew up. Right then I couldn't believe that I'd tried to actually shoot this guy. I knew I was acting like a dumb, crazy-ass kid so I abandoned that mission. Every time I saw him after that, I just walked past him.

I wasn't finished making bad decisions, though. One time, I tried to buy an eight ball (an eighth of an ounce of cocaine) so I could sell it. I was with some partners of mine in Binghampton, the same Memphis neighborhood where Anfernee "Penny" Hardaway is from. That hood is full of ruthless niggas, so I should have known some drama was bound to happen. After we got the eight ball, I went with some of my homies to sell the dope. One of them jumped into a car near us with the people who were supposed to be buying it.

At first, it was just supposed to be a quick sale, but they started fighting in the car and took off with the drugs and the money. We were asking each other why they were driving off. They were trying to rob us, so we started trailing them. We caught up to them and I jumped out of the car as I saw them reaching under their seats. I thought they were going for their guns, so I pulled a gun on the guy and let off a couple shots.

Squeezing the trigger made me feel like a totally different person, like I was ready to kill somebody. I felt like I blacked out for a second. All the fear in my body left and everything slowed down. When I got my bearings back, we heard the police coming, so we drove off. The robbers did, too. With the police on their way, there was no reason to chase them. I knew this wasn't for me. The robbers got away with the drugs and the money.

I wasn't ready to totally give up the streets, though. Another bad decision I made was I started to hang around the wrong type of people. I'd go to people's houses, drink, smoke weed, and hang out.

But I always ended up getting back to music. Like many kids, I was in the high school band. I played the big bass drum. Although Pat wasn't in the band, he played violin.

I told my high school music teacher that I was working on music. Incredibly, he told me that he had a four-track but that he never did anything with it. Because I was working at Kroger, I was able to save up some money. My teacher Coach Jefferson sold me his TASCAM four-track for $100. It was a little beat-up, but it was all I had and all I needed.

My parents didn't really understand, appreciate, or believe in what I was working on, but they knew I was working hard. "Boy, you be on that four-track all day," my mom would say to me. I'll never forget what my dad said to me: "You think there's going to be one person holding a golden rock and they're going to throw it out into the crowd of 200 people. You think you're going to be the one to catch that golden rock?"

"Yes," I said.

He dismissed me. "Boy," he told me, "you're living in a fantasy world. That music stuff ain't nothing. You think you're going to make it in music? Forget it. Give it up." My parents didn't believe in me and wanted me to just get a job, go to college—just do anything but music.

I didn't really care what my parents said. I could rap, scratch. I felt like they simply didn't know how good I was. They just didn't get it. They were old and out of touch. But their doubt made me feel like an underdog, that no one could see my talent.

Then one of my homeboys introduced me to D Magic, who had all this DJ equipment. I was about 16 and he was like 35. He lived down the street from me on Evergreen in a shotgun house right in front of the dope spot. If you walked out of his place, there'd be dealers serving like 20 junkies. That's why D Magic kept all his equipment in his back room.

On top of that, people from Evergreen were at war with nearby Watkins and Brown. If anyone from that hood had found out I was from Evergreen, they probably would have killed me. All I was trying to do was make music, but that didn't matter in the streets. I was claiming Evergreen. I was on Evergreen and I was hanging out with dudes from Evergreen, so I had to be very careful and keep my head on a swivel. It seemed like everyone I was around was a criminal.

When I got to his house, I noticed D Magic had the equipment I needed to be a real DJ. He had great speakers and what every DJ wanted: Technics SL-1200 turntables. These were the best on the market because they were among the world's first electronic direct-drive turntables. Instead of using a belt system to rotate the platter that would spin the vinyl, these turntables used a high-torque motor connected directly to the platter to spin the record. This change cut out belt vibrations and variations in speed that would change the pitch of the records as the DJ would cut, scratch, or blend records. The "1200s," as they were known, had a pitch adjustment dial, which made it easier to match beats as you were going from one turntable to the other. The vibration-absorbing base enabled the music to be played as loud as possible—and with heavy bass, a rap favorite—without the needle skipping. The 1200s were the Holy Grails of turntables.

D Magic gave me a record and I started scratching it. As D Magic saw me work his equipment, he was blown away, especially since I was so young, just 16. "Man. You's hard as fuck," he told me. "I'm old-school. I don't really do all that scratching, but I know that's the new thing. I've got some gigs, so why don't we start a business together? I'll hook the equipment up and you DJ, and we split the money down the middle."

That was a big change in my life. I went to my high school principal and asked to DJ the junior high dance. He told me I could, as long as I stayed out of trouble and stopped getting into so many fights. I promised him I would, so he let me. I was nervous as fuck. People were coming in and one of my homies was like, "I know you like to scratch, but just play the music. People don't want to hear all that scratching."

The reality is, though, that I didn't really know how to DJ a party. This was my first time. I'm playing music, but I'm scratching. Everyone was looking at me like I was crazy. People started saying, "Play the damn music, Jordan," calling me by my given name. Juicy J hadn't really kicked in yet. I paid attention to what they were saying and played some music, but I was still scratching a lot. It took me a little while, but I got the hang of it.

Soon afterward, D Magic and I were setting up our equipment for another dance. About 50 people had gotten to the gym early. Some were in the bleachers. Others were shooting ball. Once we finished setting up, I started scratching. I was doing the tricks Jazzy Jeff would do back in the day. I was doing tricks behind my back, scratching using my elbows. I felt like I was Q, Omar Epps' character in *Juice*. People were getting so hyped that they started screaming. People were coming up to me like, "Damn. You cold as fuck."

After that, I started getting a little name for myself and people started recognizing me as Juicy J. I started DJing dances and damn near every party in North Memphis. The streets were never too far away, though. Every time I'd DJ a party, somebody would start fighting, start shooting. I'd be DJing and ducking.

Then I started making mixtapes. I'd get $10 to make personalized mixtapes. My friends Patriece "Big Triece" Ray, Andre Wallace, and Antwan Bruce seemed genuinely happy for my success, especially when I'd say, "I've got my dog Big Triece in this muthafucka." People would hear that and want their own tape. It felt like everybody was calling me to make them a tape. I was always trying to sell my mixtapes, so I'd carry a black bag full of them. That bag and walking bowlegged became two of my trademarks.

Then I started doing little raps on the instrumental parts of the tapes. I had this song called "Criminal Zone."

"In the criminal zone," I rapped, *"everybody owns a tone."* I considered North Memphis a criminal zone because there were nothing but criminals around us. "Tone" was our slang for a gun because of the sound it made when it was fired. It seemed like everybody had one.

Like many of the rappers who came before me, I wrote about what was going on in my life, what I was seeing in my neighborhood, my city. Since I was in the criminal zone, I wrote about it. I felt like almost everyone around me was robbing, killing, stealing—and everyone, it seemed, had a gun and a jheri curl.

People heard "Criminal Zone" and were like, "Man. You be rappin', too? Damn, you're hard, dog." The song and my hype started spreading throughout the city.

My friend Ren and I had heard about this label, OTS Records. 8Ball & MJG were signed to them. So was Gangsta Pat. The label was based in Memphis, too, and it was making some noise. Ren and I heard that OTS' rapper Psycho needed a DJ, so we looked up the label's address and went to their office, which was housed in the 21st Century Community Learning Center. The facility was similar to a Boys & Girls Club. It had a basketball court and baseball and football facilities, and also a studio.

When we got to the studio, Psycho was there. So were 8Ball & MJG. Everyone there was speaking the type of pimp lingo I'd heard growing up. Then they asked us to rap. Ren got on the mic and he started rapping. I told them I could rap, but that I was really a DJ. They got the turntables and asked to see what I could do. They told me I was cold, too. I decided to rap, and they were impressed by that. They told me I rapped better than Ren.

Psycho told me that he wanted me to DJ for him when he opened for 8Ball & MJG. I did, and when 8Ball & MJG lost their DJ, I started DJing for them, too. We did shows throughout Tennessee and Mississippi. I was still in high school, and driving a Ford Fairmont. Being around 8Ball & MJG, I learned how to produce records, how to flow on the mic, and how to carry myself as a professional.

8Ball & MJG acted like brothers. I never saw them clash, and I saw how dedicated they were to their craft. They'd be working on beats and would sometimes sleep in the studio.

People would see me with 8Ball & MJG and word got out that I was coming up. I was starting to get to the level of other prominent DJs, like DJ Spanish Fly, Sonny D, and DJ Squeeky.

People loved "Criminal Zone" and I was gaining clout throughout Memphis, and I put a song out called "Don't Be Scared, Put A Rubber On The Head." When I was in twelfth grade, I'd gotten gonorrhea from this girl, which is why I made the song. Right after that, I took an HIV test, too. I was nervous for weeks, waiting on the results. Thank God it was negative. After that, every time I'd have sex, I would wear two rubbers. I also got regular checkups to make sure I was okay. People used to know me for that because I'd talk about it all the time.

You don't get any feeling with two rubbers on, but I was so nervous because there was also a lot of HIV, AIDS, STDs, and people getting burned in my high school and in the neighborhood. A friend of mine had even died of AIDS. He had come to my studio one time and couldn't even stand up. I didn't want to get that shit, so I doubled up on the condoms and went and got tested for everything. With all that going on in the streets, "Don't Be Scared, Put A Rubber On The Head" got popular in the neighborhood, too. So did my song "Slob On My Nob," which I had been hanging on to since I wrote it in eleventh grade. I recorded both of those songs on the $100 four-track recorder I bought off my teacher.

The success of these songs inspired me to put out my own mixtapes. I'd put songs from major artists such as N.W.A on there, and I'd add one or two of mine, too. This gave me recognition as a rapper.

The success made me think that I could actually get out of the hood.

Growing up with inconsistent food, no room to stretch out, and limited money gave me a hustle mentality. It also taught me to save my money and to spend it wisely. I decided to put some money in with some friends to buy drugs. They'd go buy them, sell them, and then split the profits with the people who put in money. It was good, quick money, but I knew where that type of work led you—jail or dead—so I didn't mess with that too much or for long. I was just trying to make something happen.

I was always able to walk away from a situation when I thought it was too dangerous because I felt I had a music career that was on the rise. That's why I never went too heavy in the streets.

But as I dabbled in the streets, I started gravitating toward rougher rap like N.W.A. Although DJ Jazzy Jeff & The Fresh Prince's music was dope, I felt like they were just having fun. They were making songs like "Girls Ain't Nothing But Trouble." With N.W.A, I remember on "Dopeman" how Ice Cube rapped about someone on their hands and knees searching for a piece of rock. I was blown away that he said *rock*, as in a piece of crack cocaine. I couldn't believe he said that, and that Cube knew about rock enough to rap about it.

Whether it was early in the morning or late at night, I'd see people near the Cypress Gardens Apartments where we lived in what looked like a demonic trance. They were walking around looking for rock. Unlike other drugs, crack made you *look different*. It made you fiend for another hit, like you were possessed. People were selling their houses and their cars to buy more crack and get high. Even one of the teachers I knew at Northside High School was addicted to crack. He was buying drugs from his students. I saw it destroy him. He's dead now.

Ice Cube also issued a warning on "Dopeman": don't get high on your own supply. He must have seen how even the dealers were getting hooked on this new drug. Based on what Ice Cube was rapping about, I felt like LA must be just like Memphis.

I loved the idea that they were actually talking about what was really going on in the neighborhood, like how Eazy-E opened "Boyz-N-The-Hood" by rapping: *"Cruisin' down the street in my 6-4/Jockin' the freaks, clockin' the dough."*

Ice-T, N.W.A, and Geto Boys, they were just straight raw. Willie D had the song "Bald Headed Hoes." That was like more of where I came from. I was like, "Man. I just saw a bald-headed hoe the other day. He must have been in Memphis. He must know about the hood."

I loved Public Enemy, Boogie Down Productions, KRS-

One, and X Clan. They had a message in their songs and would talk about Black power, politics, and teaching, which was pretty dope to me. Their messages were in sync with what my parents would tell my brother and sisters and me. My mom would always be like, "Vote Democrat." Part of the reason my parents pushed Democrats so hard was because President Ronald Reagan was hated in the Black community. I remember wishing that Jesse Jackson, a Black man, would beat Reagan in the 1984 election. I knew Jackson wouldn't win, though. I couldn't imagine a Black man would ever be elected President of the United States.

Some of the ideas my parents preached to my siblings and me made it into my early raps. I wanted us to stick together as Black men. I had such high hopes that if we all stood together we could win in America. That's why political rap meant so much to me. Since I saw so much violence, I thought political music might help make a change in society. It's something I thought about on a regular basis.

The songs from these Black artists were more to me than just music. Being a Black dude from the South, I wanted my businesses to be Black-owned and Black-operated. The words and messages of KRS-One pointed me in that direction. Nonetheless, I was just more attracted to Geto Boys and N.W.A. They were reflecting what I was seeing, and I felt like I could relate to more of their music. Plus, Dr. Dre was making N.W.A's beats, and I felt like nobody could fuck with him musically.

As I said, I wrote "Slob On My Nob" in the eleventh grade. I didn't have a beat for it at the time, but I wrote one verse one day and the second verse the following day. Then I looped up the beat for EPMD's "You're A Customer." I rapped to that beat. *"Slob on my nob/Like corn on the cob."* I recorded the song on that beat, but I didn't like it. I had it on a couple mixtapes, but it didn't do anything.

Later, I had a friend that had an SP-1200 drum machine and sampler. People usually only think of it as a drum machine, but it could sample, too. I'd pay my friend to let me use it. I made a drumbeat on it, the one that ended up being on "Slob On My Nob." I recorded and mixed it in my bedroom with my headphones on.

Thanks to D Magic's connections and my buzz, I got a gig DJing every Sunday at Excalibur, a club in South Memphis right next to the studio of famous trumpeter, producer, and executive Willie Mitchell. Wanting to make sure things were done to my liking, I drew the flyers promoting my appearances. One night, I played the new version of "Slob On My Nob," the one with the brand-new beat that no one had ever heard. Nobody moved. Again.

A week later, D Magic and I were back at Excalibur setting up. Somebody came up to me and said, "Yo, Juicy. Make sure you play that song you played last week." I didn't know what he was talking about. He said, "The one where you say 'Slob On My Nob.' That shit's hard." I told him the song was goofy and that I wasn't going to play it. Then, somebody else came up and asked me to play it.

I decided to play "Slob On My Nob." The crowd went *crazy*. After that, I released another mixtape. That's when I blew up. I'd gone from being just another DJ in the neighborhood to being the hottest DJ in Memphis. "Don't Be Scared, Put A Rubber On The Head" got me hot in the streets. I took off with "Slob On My Nob." It turned me into an artist. After that, I was *that dude* in the city. I had truly made a name for myself.

Even with these musical breakthroughs, I was still hanging out with the wrong crowd sometimes. I'd gotten a new car, an Oldsmobile Delta 88, but since I didn't have any credit, I put it in one of my homies' names. Then I missed payments on it, so it got repossessed. My mom loaned me some money, and I scraped up some of my own money. I went to get the car back and dude was like, "Nah. You can't get the car back. It's not in your name. If you want it, you've got to bring the person whose name is on the title with you." So I called my boy. He said he was going to call his credit company and see what's up. This dude, my boy, had his cousin call me up. She called me at my parents' house and my dad picked up. I was listening as she talked to my dad. She acted like she was from the credit union. She said I'd have to give her $500 and then he would go over and sign for the car.

I recognized her voice, so I got my rusty 9-millimeter and told my dad we were going to go have my boy sign the paper. We pulled up on him. I cocked my gun back and told him he was going to sign the paper. He signed the paper and that was that. My dad wasn't tripping. Yes, my father was a man of God, but he knew we lived in the hood and that we needed to protect ourselves. My dad felt the guy was trying to con us out of $500, and he didn't want that to happen. I got my car back and stopped messing with that group of people.

Around the same time, I was also wrestling with a painful family revelation. My mom told us kids that our dad had two daughters we never knew about. One was in St. Louis and the other was in the Maryland-Washington, D.C., area. It wasn't a long conversation, and my mom was matter-of-fact. But the shock and pain were overwhelming.

My mother was heartbroken. So was I. She didn't deserve to go through that. She was a good mother. I felt so sorry for my mom.

Before this, I looked up to my father and thought he could do no wrong. My father was a preacher, a man of God, but he fathered two kids outside of his marriage. I'd been lied to. All of us had been. My mom had known and kept it from the kids, too, which was another blow. Sooner or later, whatever is done in the dark eventually comes to the light. No matter what you do, it's coming.

As I thought back to my childhood, I wondered about all the times my dad went away, saying he was going on the road. Was he just lying to all of us? I think he would be away for so long because he had other kids and a few other women that he was messing around with.

Then a wave of memories hit me. I remembered when I was coming up that people in the neighborhood would often say to me, "Man. Your dad was over here." But they were saying it like they were joking, like they knew something that I didn't. "Yeah. He was over here, but he left."

That didn't make any sense to me. It was ratchet where I was hanging out. My dad was nothing like that. I always wondered what a preacher would be doing in that part of the hood.

I tried to figure out what was going on. I was in full-on investigation mode, but my mom didn't say anything beyond her initial statement that my dad had other children.

I felt betrayed and wanted to hold these mistakes over my father's head. Ever since I started making some money, I'd been giving my dad my tithes for the church he worked with. I stopped cold turkey because I didn't feel like he was who he said he was. I even told my mom she should divorce him. I didn't really want her to, but I was so upset.

Pat really helped me through this time. Just because you're a man of God, you're still human. We all make mistakes. Even though I thought my father was strictly by the book, Pat told me our dad wasn't God Almighty.

Pat really had to break things down for me. He explained that our dad was a good dad, that he could have just left us on the street. He could have just never come back one day. Our father loved us and took care of us, Pat stressed to me. I had to understand that. He was our father, but he wasn't perfect.

In order to vent, I referred to the situation in my song "The Notorious Juicy J" from my *Notorious Mix Tape Vol. 5.* I didn't say my dad's name, but I was dissing him on there. *"Sometime I watch TV and see that preacher shit/And just wanna kill and be rid of all hypocrites/I feel like I'm crazy 'cause the anger inside me/The shotgun is loaded, so it'll be dangerous to try me,"* I rapped on the song. You can hear the pain in my voice when I say that. That was about my dad because I didn't think he was practicing what he preached.

I felt like there was nothing I could say to my father that would make things better, so I didn't even talk to him about it. The damage was done.

I tried to forget about my dad's actions, but I was reeling from the pain my father caused my family and me. Even though I was a working DJ, my name was starting to die down a little bit. I started to wonder what was next, what I was going to do with my life. I was 21, 22. I didn't know if I could DJ forever and I was still staying at my parents' place. I felt like it was time for a change.

One guy I knew was Andre "Cash Money," one of the first people to play Three 6 Mafia's music on the radio. I told him I wanted to be a radio DJ, a personality who could mix and scratch on the air. He brushed me off. But since I was a club DJ and didn't think I could have been a radio personality, I never followed up with him. I felt like I was going nowhere.

After that, I went to Dr. Benjamin L. Hooks Job Corps Center to try to get some work, something better than Kroger or the Piggly Wiggly I had also worked at. I told my dad and he was like, "Nah. You ain't gonna like working for no other man. Just keep doing what you're doing. You've been DJing and you've been making money with that."

I knew I wasn't going to give up, but I wanted to have some money. I didn't want to get to a point where I was doing mixtapes and then the mixtapes stopped selling. Then what?

Despite my uncertainty, my dad was right. I was about to make a major breakthrough.

CHAPTER

4

TRIPLE SIX CLUBHOUSE

I WAS TIRED AND losing focus. I had started drinking more, smoking some weed, hanging out real late. I was spending time in Binghampton, a section of North Memphis with some of the city's worst criminals. Sure, I was still practicing my turntable skills and making beats at home, but I was also trying to figure out how to get into the studio for a cheaper price.

I'd also been doing some work with OTS Records, DJing for 8Ball & MJG. One of my partners who knew the guys at OTS told me I should connect with a guy named DJ Paul who I'd been hearing about. Paul lived on the South Side and had been putting out mixtapes, too. He'd been putting out the *Killa Mix* mixtapes series and would be rapping about devil shit. I'd also heard stories that Paul was DJing from a wheelchair and that his arm was messed up, but my partner told me that Paul and I would make some dope music. So he put Paul and me on the phone, and then I went by Paul's house. I had no idea what type of dude I was about to meet.

Paul's father owned a pest control company. Paul and his family lived in this big-ass house right around the corner from Elvis Presley's house. It was a real nice neighborhood. They had like four or five bedrooms in the house. Paul had his own bedroom and another room in the house that was his studio. He also had his own car, and his mother wasn't pressing him about going to school.

I thought Paul was rich. Later Paul told me that he thought that I'd come in like some crazy lunatic and shoot up the place since I was from North Memphis. Paul had good reason to believe that.

People from North Memphis didn't like people from South Memphis. The sections of the city always seemed to be at war with one another, a reality that went back to at least the 1960s. I knew people from North Memphis who wouldn't even go to South Memphis. That's how serious it was.

I wasn't like that, though, and being in a house like Paul's was like a different world. I was coming from a two-bedroom apartment with six people. Sometimes we didn't have food. Paul lived a very different reality. It looked like he had everything: keyboards, an expensive four-track recorder, a mic booth. Yes, Paul's arm was deformed, but he could play piano and scratch so I never looked at him differently or strangely because of it. Plus, he was super smart and a good business partner who was really good at math and numbers.

When I first met Paul, though, I thought it was kind of weird that he used to walk around with a doll of Chucky, the star of the *Child's Play* movies. He also had Chucky spray-painted on the back of his car.

Paul's nonmusical interests meant little to me. I felt like a weirdo, too. Sometimes, I'd even use a cane to walk, like I was some type of pimp even though I wasn't. I never had any aspirations to have women work for me. I just wanted to be fly and a player with the ladies. We all had our quirks and were starting to develop our respective images.

In our music, we both talked about what was going on in our neighborhoods, but my stuff had a lot of soul samples, too. My vibe was Playboy Juice, a player from the North Side, while Paul focused on wild, street stuff. Paul and I started making beats together. Other times I'd give him some money and rent out his studio, fuck with his Roland W-30 keyboard a little bit. Paul didn't have just any four-track, either. He had one that cost $1,000. It was light-years better than the one I'd been using. He also had a professional microphone. I'd never seen anybody with that much equipment at their house.

Right out the gate, Paul and I worked well together. I'd give him ideas and he would program the drum patterns and music. Other times, I'd make beats on the SP-1200 my friend had or a stolen Akai MPC60 I'd bought off someone for $100. I still have that MPC60. This is how we started.

Paul and I quickly became good friends. In 1993, we started a group called Backyard Posse. Less than a year later, we formed Triple Six Mafia with Paul's nephew Lord Infamous. Most people think that Paul and Lord are brothers, but they're not. Paul's older sister is Lord's mother, so Paul and Lord are actually uncle and nephew.

In one of his early raps, Lord Infamous had said, "Triple six thugs." We were a clique, like a mafia, and that's how we came up with the Triple Six Mafia name. Lord Infamous was very creative. He referred to himself as "The Scarecrow," and fans knew him for his wicked rhymes. But when I first met him, he was a quiet, chill dude. When he did talk, he'd want to discuss the earth, the moon, the stars, and God. For some reason, he was always drinking milk. Unlike so many people I knew, he wasn't on drugs, either.

The three of us were tight, but then the crew grew to like 20 people. We had Gangsta Blac, Playa Fly, Lil' Glock & S.O.G., Lil Noid, Koopsta Knicca, La Chat, Gangsta Boo, Crunchy Black, my friend Ren, Lil' E, Wicked, my brother, Patrick, aka Project Pat. (A guy Pat knew named him Project Pat because every time the guy said he saw Pat, he was in the projects.)

After a while, Paul and I narrowed it down to six people who we felt were the hardest. Of course, DJ Paul, Lord Infamous, and I were going to be in the group. The other three were Gangsta Boo, Crunchy Black, and Koopsta Knicca. Everybody who wasn't in Triple Six Mafia would be pushed as a solo artist, from Playa Fly and Gangsta Blac to Project Pat and La Chat.

As for the group, Gangsta Boo was an amazing rapper and a real hood chick. She was younger than everybody. I was blown away that a female could come with lyrics like that. Her talent was amazing. It added some extra sauce to the group.

I'd known Crunchy before I knew Paul. I met Crunchy at the 21st Century Community Learning Center, where I'd also met 8Ball & MJG. Crunchy and his girlfriend would dress alike, everything from matching overalls to shoes. They were dancers. He was cool, chill, and would dance for pioneering Memphis rapper Al Kapone. I hadn't seen him in a while, but when Paul put him down with the crew, Crunchy had gotten more into the streets and doing hood shit. He had a totally different vibe now, Killa Crunchy. He wasn't really a rapper, so he didn't even rap on our first mixtape, 1994's *Smoked Out Loced Out*. He was just our dancer at first.

I really liked what Crunchy added to the group. Having someone onstage doing Memphis dances, including the gangster walk, was different in that era. Crunchy also served as a bodyguard of sorts for Paul. Another one of his responsibilities was to keep our guns ready, which was important.

As we were forming the group, my sister Cheryl reminded me that Koopsta Knicca and I had gone to the same high school. I hadn't looked at him as important, so I'd actually forgotten about him. Then I remembered that Big Triece and I actually had a class with him and that every now and then Koopsta would try to talk to me about rapping. He was too weird to me, though, so I would ignore him. When I saw him, I'd walk right past him. That was then. When Koopsta joined the crew, I wanted to make things work, so I left all that in the past. He had a scary voice, which he showcased on his great underground mixtape *The Devil's Playground* that he made with Paul. He started off as one of the hardest rappers in Triple Six Mafia.

The six of us—DJ Paul, Lord Infamous, Gangsta Boo, Crunchy Black, Koopsta Knicca, and I—got into a good workflow immediately. DJ Paul and I were the producers and I looked at Lord Infamous as the main rapper. He was the star of Triple Six Mafia. Lord could rap and sing, and he had crazy melodies. Most importantly, we were all on the same page and everybody was pouring their ideas into Triple Six Mafia. If what I had sounded good, things went my way. If somebody else had a better idea, we went their way. We were all team players, all in it for the betterment of Triple Six Mafia. For the first time in a long time, I had hope. I thought we were building the next big thing out of Memphis.

Paul and I loved the dark, demonic vibe. We worked on that together. However, I explored my other creative sides, too. I would experiment with jazz sounds and would sample Motown singer Willie Hutch. I was really big on experimentation and trying different things. Every time I made a beat, I would change something, maybe the snare. I would make a dark beat, but then I'd grab a sample from some bright-ass sound. I would sample a song from a soul artist, but I would put a street hook on the song. On my *Volume No. 7* mixtape in 1993, I had the song "Bring It On," which samples Al Green's song "Jesus Is Waiting." On one of Project Pat's mixtapes (and again on his album *Ghetty Green*), we made "Niggas Got Me Fucked Up," which samples Isaac Hayes' "Make A Little Love To Me." A prominent example of this later in our career is Three 6 Mafia's 2005 hit single "Poppin' My Collar," which samples Willie Hutch's "Theme Of The Mack." This formula worked time and time again.

As Paul, Lord Infamous, and I were developing our relationship, I was feeling pressure from what seemed like everywhere. I wanted to escape the evil, escape the streets, stop having to deal with phony-ass people, and make a better way for myself, so in 1993 I made a tape called *Escape From Hell*. It had several meanings. The other Triple Six Mafia members talked about Hell so much (DJ Paul and Lord Infamous even had a mixtape called *Come w/Me 2 Hell*) and I felt like I was already living in Hell in North

Memphis. I was so tired of what was happening that I used *Escape From Hell* to vent, to diss people who had pissed me off.

One of the dudes I rapped about was bigger than me. Everyone was afraid of him, but I didn't give a fuck. One day I'd been talking shit to this dude—crazy enough, it was the same guy that introduced me to DJ Paul—in the parking lot of this club. When I went inside, he shot out my car window, jumped in his car, and drove off. I thought he really wasn't trying to shoot me. He was just trying to scare me.

That didn't matter in a lot of ways, though. People had seen the incident, which made it worse. I felt like I was in a situation where I was going to have to kill this guy. In Memphis, you have to retaliate. If not, I was going to be looked at like a pussy-ass nigga for the rest of my life. I had to do something to him, or someone else was going to try me to see if they could get away with it, too. When I told Pat about what had happened, he told me, "We're gonna get him." That's all Pat said, and I knew what that meant.

Soon thereafter, Pat and I were at a party. Someone told Pat that the guy was downstairs. I tried to stop Pat from going downstairs because I knew he would shoot him, but I was too late. Fortunately, the guy saw Pat coming and ran. I really don't think this guy knew the type of people I had down with me.

As I was growing up and then getting into the Memphis music scene, I had seen so much dirt that I decided not to let people know too much about me. People didn't know where I lived. They didn't know Project Pat was my brother. They didn't know who I was friends with.

I wasn't coming around like I was some super gangster, though. I was all about business. But when somebody would come at me on some tough guy shit, I responded in kind. I'd think about Malcolm X's famous slogan in times like these. He said Black people in America wanted freedom, justice, and equality by any means necessary. Malcolm wasn't going to just sit by and let someone get over on him, or kill him. I had the same mentality. Things would have to be handled by any means necessary.

I started getting messages that the guy who shot out my car window was sorry about what happened, that he was on coke that day. As mad as I was, I wanted to leave the situation alone. Pat didn't feel the same way. He and one of his friends had gotten masked up—put ski masks on—one night and were ready to go kill the guy. They were on their way out the door when the phone rang. Pat picked the phone up. It was the guy he was about to go kill. "I'm really sorry. I apologize," the guy was pleading with Pat. "I have no problems with y'all."

Pat told me he felt like it was God intervening because he was on his way to kill this dude. It was going to happen. But that call made Pat let it go. I'm glad he did and I'm glad I did, too. Imagine what could have happened. Pat would have likely been caught and been locked up for that. I would have been at war with that guy's friends and, even worse, Pat and I might not even be here today. Had I lived but been in jail, my career almost certainly would have gone in another direction.

I was trying to escape that type of stuff, that life, so I laid low at one of my homies' houses for a while. I was having to watch my back all the time, whether I was at the gas station or pulling up to the studio. I was trying to not be robbed, not go to jail, not get beat up by the police, not get in a gun battle. People were getting kidnapped for drug money or for ransom.

My music was already dark, but after that incident, it got extra dark. I needed an outlet for my emotions, so I poured it into my beats. I was so tired of the drama. I told myself I'd hurt my enemies by getting on TV. Knowing that they'd be jealous and hurt would be the right type of payback.

One of the songs on *Escape From Hell* was "Suck A Mean Dick." That song was telling people that had a problem with me to come see me, not talk behind my back. In North Memphis, I wasn't used to people shooting in the air, shooting out car windows. We call it "pistol play" when you do that. We're used to people shooting *at* you.

I talked about some real street shit on there, but I was also trying to get right within myself. I was listening to what the Nation of Islam was teaching and would read its *The Final Call* newspaper. Although I didn't have any plans to join, I appreciated how they were Black men coming together, that they seemed to have a true brotherhood. I also gravitated further toward Malcolm X's mantra: by any means necessary. The Nation of Islam and Malcolm X didn't teach turning the other cheek, something I appreciated.

I'd even seen a brother from the Nation of Islam beat up three Black dudes at a gas station. That seemed to go against what the Nation stood for, so I asked the guy why he did it. "They're still my brothers, Brother," he said to me. "They're just lost."

But the Muslims were not into violence. They preached Black self-esteem, economic independence. Plus, they dispensed dietary advice and offered a supportive community for Black people in need.

I grew up in an all-Black neighborhood, but Memphis

was still a very racist city. Like many Black men in America, I'd gotten pulled over for a mistaken identity. I was driving in Memphis, about to make a right turn, and about four or five cop cars swarmed in on me. They pulled me out the car, slammed me on the hood, pulled guns on me. I couldn't believe what was happening, and that it was happening so fast. Then they realized I wasn't the right guy. They ran my record, realized it was clean, and were about to let me go. Then they saw I had a .38 Special on me. It was unregistered and loaded. I thought I was going to jail. But they took the bullets out, threw the gun at me, and told me, "Get a better pistol, man," before they drove off. That *Escape From Hell* album was real deep to me. I wanted to escape my reality, the Hell I felt I was living.

At the same time, Paul was rapping about being in the Gangster Disciples (GD) gang, and I think Lord Infamous was repping it, too. They would have certain things about the GDs in their lyrics, but I wasn't in a gang, so I wasn't rapping about being a gang member. I just told Paul not to throw up their signs when we were doing shows. I wanted our music to bring people together, so I didn't want us to have any problems when we were in a rival neighborhood. Paul agreed and told the whole group to leave that alone. We wanted to get money, not start fights. I was always trying to think long-range.

Lord Infamous had most of the devilish lyrics, Gangsta Boo used to call herself "The Devil's Daughter," and the group rapped a lot about doing drugs. People loved that, when we'd rap about smoking weed. I was rapping about all that, as well as some political stuff and North Memphis shit, like: *"It's the Glock that'll get your ass popped."* People loved our robbery songs, too. It was good that we had different styles. It distinguished everybody. It was a mixture and just came out dope.

Initially, I liked the name Triple Six Mafia because it sounded crazy and because it matched the vibe of our music with all the killing and robbing we rapped about. It's some evil, dark, demonic shit, and it matched what was going on in Memphis.

We also imagined that people would hear the name and be like, "What the fuck?!? Who are these guys?" I looked at the name Triple Six Mafia as a gimmick. I didn't look at it like, "Ah, man. It's the Devil." I never saw anybody worship the Devil or anything like that, but as we were using it and gaining popularity, I felt like we'd have to change the name. If we wanted to go to the next level, we couldn't use Triple Six Mafia.

We were getting a lot of doors slammed in our faces, people wouldn't play our music on the radio, and some journalists questioned us because everybody was scared to fuck with the Triple Ssix Mafia. I wanted us—and I looked at us as able—to have a bigger audience. To me, we were going to be as big as—and mysterious as—Michael Jackson or Prince. Not only that, we were also going to win Grammys.

When I would say "Triple Six Mafia," I'd see the number three in my head. It was the same for six. Since triple and three are similar, we decided in 1995 to change the name to Three 6 Mafia. Three 6 Mafia didn't sound as bad as Triple Six Mafia to people. It also read and looked better, and we were trying to get away from people thinking of us and our name as six six six, the sign of the Devil. After we changed our name, some people would even say "Thirty 6 Mafia" because they misread it. Regardless, problems with the name faded quickly once we changed it. People didn't seem to be scared anymore.

To keep things simple for the media, we came up with a reason for the name change that also happened to be true. The group started out with three people. Then we added three more. It was three of us, then six of us. Three 6 Mafia. That really helped shut down the bad press and helped people feel comfortable around us.

The name change solved a big problem. Now I was thinking about how we could expand and take what we were doing to another level. We were getting hot and our name was blowing up.

As much as I tried to get Project Pat to rap, he never seemed interested. He had talent, whether it was writing a hook or a whole song. That's a rare skill for an artist to have, to be able to write a song from start to finish, from the concept to the completion. Pat could do it, though. He was such a beast with his writing abilities and his wordplay. I'd been telling him that for years. We'd been making music together since I first started making tapes at our apartment as teenagers. But Pat was running the streets so much and getting into more and more trouble.

I'll never forget getting my first phone call about Pat. I was down the street in front of my grandmother's house, leaning on my Oldsmobile Delta 88 with gold rims and candy paint. I was talking to this girl, trying to smash. My big box cell phone rang. It was my mother. It didn't matter what I was doing—having sex, recording a song—if my mom called, I answered. Things were so bad in Memphis, I always wanted to be there in case she needed me.

When I answered, my mom told me that Pat, who was working at an office where the employees were allegedly fixing computers but were really scamming people, was in jail. Pat had smoked some Angel Dust with one of his co-workers and robbed a store in the Mall of Memphis.

Immediately I jumped in the car and drove straight home. We called it a "family alert." Whenever we got one of those, we had to go home, quickly. Our entire family was devastated and confused. My parents were going crazy. My mom kept saying, "There's something wrong with him." It was all bad.

I was hurt, but I was mad at *him*. Pat was so smart but was acting so stupidly. I felt like I had to be around him to help him get his mind right. When I was with him, I'd always tell him what we needed to be working on, to think about what he was doing and the consequences of his actions.

My dad had to scrape up money for bail and for a lawyer. I wasn't with that. I felt like Pat had gotten himself into that situation, so he should get himself out.

When we bailed Pat out of jail, he was acting extra wild. He even turned it up a notch, becoming more violent and more unpredictable. Coming up in the neighborhood, people are often faced with tough decisions and are put in tough circumstances. Someone might get jumped so many times or become so stressed out because they don't have any money that one day they wake up and are tired of it. It's like Pat went from giving a damn to not giving a fuck about anyone or anything. I felt like he was ready to go to war with everybody. It was outrageous. The neighborhood had taken Pat over.

Yeah, the neighborhood had gotten the better of me, but I never let it take me over like it did with Pat. He had gotten to the point where he'd do things and not think about them, like running up in the mall and robbing people. That wasn't how I was moving. I always tried to think things through. More than ever, I felt I really needed to keep an eye out for Pat. He seemed lost.

At the same time, I was also trying to recruit my sisters to be rappers with me, and even wrote some rhymes for them. I told Cheryl she could be the rapper and that Carol could be the DJ. I wanted all of us to be in music together. They tried, but it wasn't really for them. They were smart and on the honor roll and had other interests.

As I was getting deeper and deeper into music, I didn't focus as much on my sisters and what was going on in their lives. I made sure they were safe, but beyond that, I was so focused on what I wanted to be and what I wanted to do that I drifted away from them. My mom wouldn't let them go anywhere, other than maybe one of our cousins' houses. Memphis was a rough city and my mom was trying to keep my sisters safe from the outside world. In the back of my mind, I wanted to be able to get my sisters—and the rest of my family—out of the hood.

As I poured more and more of myself into my music, my beats were sounding better and better. Project Pat had been coming up with these crazy flows and talking realistic street shit. There were times where I'd talk about shooting someone in the face in a song, but I'd never done that. Rap was rap. Sometimes we talked about things we did. Sometimes it was just rapping. But once Pat got out of jail, everything he was rapping about was real. I knew. I saw him going through it. That's when we did his *Murderers & Robbers* mixtape, which got his name buzzing throughout the city.

On the title track, Pat even referenced the time the guy shot out my car window: *"Niggas trip me out always trying* to play hard/Ridin' around the hood shootin' up a nigga's car/A car ain't alive and a car ain't the nigga/You sayin' I'mma die, muthafucka pull the trigga." Project Pat was keeping it all the way real.

After the guy heard it, word got back to Pat and me that he was talking shit. We sent word back that he didn't even know what he had coming to him. We were about the business. He must have realized his potential predicament, so he started apologizing to us again.

At the same time, I didn't work with DJ Paul every day, so I was still in the streets more than I should have been. But I knew I couldn't make any money in jail or if I was dead. Yeah, I was determined to make it in music, but it wasn't easy. I was hanging out with 8Ball & MJG but still had a regular life. I was trying to smash a chick, trying to flip a buck by putting money in to buy dope. Despite being a hood celebrity, I was still in the streets like everybody else.

8Ball & MJG built a significant buzz, so upstart Houston label Suave Records—which changed its name to Suave House Records a couple years later—signed them back in 1993. Since Suave was based in Houston, 8Ball & MJG soon moved to Texas. I stayed in Memphis.

When 8Ball was back in town, people in the city were mesmerized that he had a Chevy Suburban with candy paint. That's how broke and small-minded we were. Having a nice, new Chevy was our idea of making it.

I had been dreaming of breaking through like 8Ball & MJG had. They'd signed to a label and were doing it bigger than anyone else I knew. Three 6 Mafia was about to join them.

CHAPTER

5

WHERE DA CHEESE AT

THREE 6 MAFIA STARTED off better than most groups. One store, Pop Tunes, called us because people would be coming in the record store looking for our mixtapes on cassette. We worked out a deal with Pop Tunes where we'd sell them the tapes on consignment. For every sale, we'd get $3 profit. So, we'd bring 100 over there, and they'd sell out in less than an hour. We'd have to re-up like this on a regular basis. We did the same thing at custom car shops, like TNT Pro Audio and Mr Z Sound Express, where people would go to get high-end stereos and upholstery for their rides. We were making really good money, a couple thousand here, a couple thousand there.

We were able to enjoy our newfound wealth, too. We bought really nice cars and got gold rims. We were living good off the mixtapes.

We were acting as our own record company, as well as

our own distributor. We'd go get the tapes, print up the info, put the stickers on them, and drop them off at various stores in Memphis. Since we were selling hundreds of mixtapes weekly at Pop Tunes alone, word got out about us to one of the biggest players in the city. Select-O-Hits, a major Memphis-based regional music distribution company, reached out to Pop Tunes, and that's how we got connected. They knew our mixtapes and independent projects were selling out at local record stores.

When Sam Phillips launched Sun Records in 1952 in Memphis, he began his ascent in the music industry. The legendary label released early material from such Black musicians as Johnny London, Joe Hill Louis, and Willie Nix, as well as White ones such as Elvis Presley, Johnny Cash, Carl Perkins, Roy Orbison, and Jerry Lee Lewis, among others. Seven years later, Sam's brother Tom Phillips (who had been a former manager of Lewis) founded Select-O-Hits. It operated out of Sun Records' original warehouse and evolved over the years, adapting to changes in the independent music marketplace. Select-O-Hits had its hands in warehousing product and helping independent labels at retail. It also acted as a "one-stop," essentially a middleman between upstart record companies and record stores. "One-stops" would buy albums and singles from major and independent labels and then sell the product to chain, independent, and other retail outlets in their region.

When Tom stepped down in 1979, he left the business to three of his children: president Skip Phillips, vice president Johnny Phillips, and administrative assistant Kathy Gordon. The business thrived under their lead. That same year, Select-O-Hits found its niche: distribution. By 1986, Select-O-Hits was the Mid-South distributor for such record companies as Fantasy, Malaco, Alligator, Select, and Tommy Boy. Malaco, for instance, was the initial distributor of Eazy-E's Ruthless Records and its landmark 1987 single "Boyz-N-The-Hood." In other words, Select-O-Hits was a major player in the independent music scene that was right in our backyard.

Johnny Phillips wanted to meet with us. When Paul and I went to their office, Johnny told us that his son was listening to our music. We could hardly believe it. Our music was already getting out of the hood, even in Memphis.

During our visit, I liked Johnny's vibe. He's from Memphis and understood music. Johnny told us that he loved what we were doing and that we had developed a buzz on our own. *He* took us around his warehouse and showed us all the records Select-O-Hits was distributing. I had no idea they were distributing Eazy-E's material as well as Priority Records' other releases. Select-O-Hits was massive. I was thinking, "These guys discovered Elvis. Now they want to work with Three 6 Mafia. Who knows what could happen?"

Given the buzz we had in the streets, Select-O-Hits said we could do one of two different kinds of deals, an artist deal or a press and distribution deal, known in the industry as a P&D deal. I appreciated that Johnny respected us and wasn't trying to take over what we were doing. As I would later find out, it was rare for a successful person in the music industry to let you run your own ship and retain complete ownership of your music.

Paul and I read over both deals. I also spoke about the opportunity with Project Pat, who was in jail at the time. I didn't really run all the numbers against our expectations, because we didn't think we'd sell too many copies.

But with the P&D deal, we knew we'd get 90 percent of the net profit per CD sold. That sounded promising. Plus, we wouldn't just be artists signed to somebody. We would be coming in as businessmen and owning our own label. I wanted to be like Stax, and this was a way to do it.

After Paul, Pat, and I discussed the deals, we realized we wanted to do our own thing. At first, I came up with Paul and Juicy Records. It was corny, so we ended up settling on Prophet Entertainment and agreed to a P&D deal with Select-O-Hits. That was the beginning of our record label and being CEOs. We were so hands-on. Paul drew the Prophet Entertainment logo and, later, the one for our label Hypnotize Minds, too.

We were starting to make a name for ourselves, but we weren't at the Stax level yet. We had some money, but not *crazy* money. Going to the studio was expensive, so I made a critical decision. I sold my cherished Delta 88, the one with gold rims, for studio time. I'd bought that car with the money I'd made DJing and selling my own mixtapes. I sold it for $3,000 and I bought another, cheaper Delta 88 for $1,200. A lot of people in my neighborhood thought I was going broke, but I didn't give a fuck. I had to make the right business decision. People started talking shit about me, saying I was weird, that I didn't fuck with them. They were right. I didn't.

More importantly, I didn't care because I was doing my own thing. My grandmother had always told me not to worry about people who weren't helping me put food on my table. That stuck in my head. Project Pat was locked up at the time and his car was just sitting in the driveway, so he told me I could sell his car, too. I sold both cars and put the money on studio time. It was the best investment I made in my life.

That's when we did our first album, 1995's *Mystic Stylez*, and officially launched our own record label, Prophet Entertainment. Our music had really started off hardcore and underground, and we had the riotous "Break Da Law '95,'" the robbery song "Gotta Touch 'Em (Pt. 2)," and the street-centered "In Da Game."

Around this time, we were upset with Bone thugs-n-harmony because it sounded to us like they were using the Memphis styles and flows from Lord Infamous and Koopsta Knicca in their music. Bone, who was from Cleveland and backed by Eazy-E, broke through in 1994 with the single "Thuggish Ruggish Bone" and the EP *Creepin on Ah Come Up*. That's why we dissed Bone on the *Mystic Stylez* song "Live By Yo Rep." Lord Infamous went hard on that song. *"I shall take a thousand razor blades and press them in their flesh (Damn),"* he rapped. *"Take my pitchfork out the fire, soak it in their chest."* We were not playing.

It wasn't just Bone, though. When I heard how Biggie Smalls had sampled Mtume's "Juicy Fruit" song for his single "Juicy," I thought Biggie might have heard my mixtapes. The reason I thought this was because I was calling myself The Notorious Juicy J on my mixtapes, even before he started calling himself The Notorious B.I.G. On one of my mixtapes, I even used the "Juicy Fruit" beat and scratched my name, "Juicy," in it, too. Our music was popular in Memphis, but I knew people in other cities were hearing it, too. Now, I'm not saying Biggie took anything from me, but I *felt* like he did.

We didn't want *Mystic Stylez* to be all buck and angry, though, so we did the song "Da Summa." It was a different sound, a little more laid-back, and not nearly as aggressive and confrontational. Paul started off the song reflectively, talking about how we came up. We've got Ann Hines singing the chorus. Lord Infamous and Koopsta Knicca were flowing slower, so it was easier for everyone to enjoy. I was talking about hollering at girls and the homies I grew up with. It was a different approach for us because we tried to make a song for the radio. We wanted to soothe the listener. It worked. "Da Summa" was the first Three 6 Mafia song that got some local radio play.

We tried to get a label to sign us, but no one was interested. Paul and I paid our way to go to New York and met with Fab 5 Freddy, who was working with Pallas Records at the time. They had signed Erule and Bushwackass but were really making noise with Chicago rap group Crucial Conflict and their hit single "Hay."

Fab 5 Freddy was real cool, just like he was when he was hosting *Yo! MTV Raps*. He said he really liked us and even came to Memphis to check us out in our natural element. We took him to Denim and Diamonds, a legendary club in South Memphis, and had a great time. He liked our music and was feeling our vibe, but Pallas was only offering artist deals, not like the P&D deal we had with Select-O-Hits. We wanted more than what Pallas was offering, so we didn't move forward with them.

When I would happen to see 8Ball when he was back in town, I'd tell him about *Mystic Stylez*, how Three 6 Mafia wanted to do a song with MJG and him, and that we wanted to sign with Suave Records, too. 8Ball & MJG were really putting Memphis on the map and I was happy for them, but nothing happened as a result of those early conversations.

Undeterred, we poured all our energy into the momentum we had generated locally. I looked at DJ Paul and me like we were the dynamic duo. Nobody could fuck with us musically or creatively. As rappers, everyone in Three 6 Mafia felt like their styles were different, which is why we called the album *Mystic Stylez*. Prophet Entertainment got its name playing off of the album title, too. Plus, Memphis was a dark city and we were on some dark, scary shit. We were some vicious muthafuckas with a demonic vibe rapping about robbery, murder, and people getting shot.

You could hear me breathing in the background of a lot of our songs. I came up with that idea because back in the day when somebody wanted to threaten you or spook you out over the phone, they'd call you and talk shit to you without identifying themselves. Other times, they'd call and not say anything, but you could hear them breathing. Spike Lee portrayed that in his 1992 movie *Malcolm X*. It was also similar to Jason's signature sounds from the *Friday the 13th* series.

I remember I did that one day, but the person I did it to called the police. They traced the phone to my parents' place and then went to my grandmother's house looking for me since I had called and threatened to kill the person. But that's what I would do, so I just added that element to my music, putting it in while I was rapping my verses. I also added stomps, which made it seem like I was coming after you. I was fascinated with that vibe, so I incorporated it into Three 6 Mafia's sound. Paul added in his elements and mixed them into the musical pot. It was an organic process.

Since we were trying to build a musical movement, we also featured some of the other artists we were working with on *Mystic Stylez*. We put La Chat, Lil Fly, and M.C. Mack on the title track, and Lil Fly on "Now I'm Hi Pt. 3."

We thought we'd put together a genius-level album of reality rap, but we had no idea what *Mystic Stylez* was going to do. Three 6 Mafia just wanted to put out an album. With the success of "Da Summa," we felt like we were taking it to the next level. We were on CD, in record stores, and had retail muscle because of Select-O-Hits. We felt like we were going nationwide.

After that, our music started selling like crazy. I was in a Cat's Music record store one day with my friend Big Bump. He was like, "Your shit is on the Billboard charts." I didn't know what a Billboard chart was. He showed me that we were No. 15 with a bullet on one of the charts for new and emerging artists. I didn't know what that meant. "That means you're selling some records," Big Bump told me. So I called Johnny Phillips at our distributor Select-O-Hits, asking how many records we'd sold. They told us we'd done more than 15,000 and we were still selling. I'm adding it up in my head like, "That's 15,000 copies times 90 percent of net profit per CD... Oh shit! We finna get paid!"

This first taste of real success made me feel like I was on my way to becoming my version of Al Bell from Stax Records. Paul and I started strategizing the next moves for Prophet Entertainment. We looked at ourselves as legit businessmen, because we were writing checks and planning a release schedule for our label. We started looking into getting our own office, our own studio. I wanted to get a building and put our name on it. Paul thought about a downside to that idea: whenever people would find our office, they'd shoot it up because of jealousy. He was right. That's how it was in Memphis, so I abandoned that dream.

We ended up getting our own studio, Hypnotize Minds,

in Memphis. It was located in a law office building, but we didn't put our name on the building for precautionary reasons. We also had a wrought iron door, cameras, and security upstairs and downstairs. I felt like we were really doing something, which made getting up every day and going to work easy. I felt a sense of pride in that.

My dreams were coming true, which led to more dreams. I wanted to produce R&B, and rock. Additionally, I wanted to produce movies. Now that I had my opportunity, I wanted to push even harder to get to the next level.

I still wanted to shine, though, so I did. Every time I'd get a new car I'd ride through the neighborhood with the windows down, hanging out the window. I had a brand-new Lexus and I wanted people to see me. Paul and the rest of them would get their windows tinted. I'd worked too hard for this. I wanted people to see me coming around Evergreen, cruising with the seat back. People would be screaming, "Jordan got a new car," every time I came through. I did that throughout my career, whether I was driving my new Cadillac, Bentley, Maybach, Rolls-Royce. I loved riding through the hood with my windows down, waving at people, blowing the horn. I didn't stop too often, though, because people would try to rob you. It was still North Memphis.

Our city was rallying behind us, and we ended up doing a show off Millbranch Road with Bone thugs-n-harmony during the *Mystic Stylez* run. Bone was one of the biggest groups in rap at the time and was riding high with their "1st of Tha Month" single. But when they got onstage, it seemed like the whole crowd was booing them. Three 6 Mafia weren't the only ones that thought Bone had stolen our style. The entire city did.

It looked like a riot was about to start, so Bone's security stopped the show and got them off the stage. Then someone swung at one of the Bone members, so they left the club before anything happened. We didn't exchange words with them backstage. That was just Memphis standing up for Memphis.

A year or so later, we ended up seeing Bone at the airport. They asked if we had anything to smoke. We got in the car, smoked some weed, and never mentioned any problems. We saw that they were cool, and that was it.

I'm glad we ended up seeing them at the airport when we did and that nothing happened between us. We ended up on the same label, working with Bone, doing records with them, and becoming friends.

Not all of my beefs worked out so smoothly. I was about to find out what it's like to really get played.

CHAPTER

6

WHO RUN IT

PAUL AND I DID all of the managing, wrote the contracts, set up photo shoots, handled the accounting, booked
all the shows, and did the taxes. We answered the phones
ourselves. We'd be the ones driving to our shows. We did
everything. I loved doing everything because I felt like I
was looking out for the team. But there were risks operat-
ing like this, which I also thought about.

Sometimes I'd ride through my hood in Evergreen and
just give some of my friends from the neighborhood money,
a hundred here, a couple hundred there. "Look, I might
need you to do something for me one day, a job or something," I'd tell them. "This is to let you know I'm serious,"
I'd say as I handed them the money. It was a retainer of
sorts in case things got ugly.

I wasn't trying to be on some John Gotti shit, but I had
to protect what we had going on. I also had my family, and

money was starting to stack up. Dealing with Memphis and money, I'd seen too many things go the wrong way due to jealousy or people being set up.

One time, I did get set up. I'd gone over to this girl's house. I had this two-door Chevy with a messed-up transmission, so it wouldn't go in reverse. Because of that, I always had to park it sideways. I was at the girl's crib, kicking it, and I went to sleep for a long time. I was knocked the fuck out. As I was coming to, I was thinking to myself, "Man. I've never slept that hard." I know I had a couple drinks and the girl and I had sex, but something wasn't adding up.

As I was coming to, I went straight to my pockets. All my money was gone. I went outside and all my tires were flat. I thought somebody must have put something in my drink and slashed my tires. But they didn't cut my tires. They just let the air out of them.

"I didn't have anything to do with it," the girl said over and over. I'd been sleeping in her room, so I didn't believe her. I played it cool, though. One of her brothers helped me get an air pump so I could inflate my tires. I drove off and never called her again. I didn't care about the car or the money. They were just things. I was just happy to get out of there alive.

The girl kept calling me. Finally, I answered. "You don't call me anymore. You must think I set you up," she said.

"You did, goddamn it," I told her, and hung the phone up.

I'm glad this happened because I'd learned my lesson: I wasn't ever going to sleep at a girl's house. After that, I started taking chicks to motels. I'd get a two- or three-hour motel, fuck her real quick, and drop her off at her house. I was going to do everything possible to make sure I didn't get set up and robbed again.

That's why I just always kept it business with people. I was dealing with a lot of hood people so I always thought about what I would do if I were in their situation. If I was at my lowest, I'd probably rob someone if I could get away with it or shoot someone if they stole from me.

But I wasn't doing anyone dirty. I was always honest with people. I'd say, "This is your contract. This is how much you get. This is what we spent." Every artist would get a statement, a check in the mail. Paul and I handled everything up front and straight up. Everything was fair. I stand on the business. If I do a deal with you, you're going to get your money whether I end up liking you or not.

We were so in-house that I used to have this big-ass briefcase (a nod to my father and his briefcase) with all of our checks. I would keep it with me at all times with the checks in it.

Even though we kept everything in-house so we wouldn't succumb to outside forces, our success was met with almost immediate drama. One of our protégés Lil Fly had been one of my best friends. We'd hang out, make a lot of music together, and get high as fuck. We put Lil Fly's "Slangin' Rocks (Pt. 2)" on DJ Paul's *Volume 16 "4 Da Summer Of '94"* mixtape, and he also appeared on *Breaking The Law*, an underground album from another rapper we were working with, Gangsta Blac. After the success of *Mystic Stylez* (which featured Lil Fly on two songs), we planned on putting out a Lil Fly project on Prophet Entertainment.

With Lil Fly's buzz and what we were already building with Three 6 Mafia, I thought we'd be able to build

Prophet Entertainment into a force right out the gate and get paid.

But I heard Lil Fly and his dad weren't happy with DJ Paul. I wasn't exactly sure what was going on between Paul and Fly, but he was about to make his feelings known.

Lil Fly changed his name to Playa Fly and dropped his *Just Gettin' It On* underground album while *Mystic Stylez* was still making waves. *Just Gettin' It On* had the streets of Memphis on fire thanks to the song "Triple Bitch Mafia," where he was dissing us. There wasn't a killing vibe to the song, though. He was just saying some stuff.

Even after Playa Fly dissed us on "Triple Bitch Mafia," I didn't care. I knew what type of dude he was, where his heart was. I knew his dad, his family. In order to try to fix things between Playa Fly and Three 6 Mafia, I went by myself to his house. "You're hot now," I told him. "Let's do a contract. I know you're dissing us, but that ain't shit."

Playa Fly and his dad wanted to work with us, but they had some deep issues with Paul. In addition to their initial rift, they had also heard Paul was bootlegging Playa Fly's *Just Gettin' It On*. I told Playa Fly and his dad that we could figure it out and work through the issue, but they would only work with me.

With all the drama with Playa Fly, I never really looked at it like it was just him. It was more of the entourage, the people around him and us that caused the rift. When we'd hear that people were dissing us, we'd listen to the tapes and try to figure out the voices we didn't know. We felt like those were the people we had to watch out for, not the rapper. The rap stuff was phony to me anyway, just a way for artists to bring attention to themselves.

One time my demon side took over, though. Three 6

Mafia was doing a show and Playa Fly jumped onstage. I threw him off the stage, grabbed my chrome Smith & Wesson .357 with hollow-point bullets, and told everybody to leave the club. I was really ready to go to war. That really wasn't in my character, but Playa Fly had pushed me to the edge by constantly talking shit.

After we got out of the club, I was driving away with my gun on my lap. I didn't underestimate the people that he was around. The guy who'd DJ'd the event called me, telling me that they had me on camera waving my gun around in the club and that the police were coming to get me. I was so mad and still on demon time. "Fuck you and fuck that club." I told the dude, "I'm rich. If they lock me up, I'll be out in less than 24 hours," and hung up the phone.

At the time, I was living in a house I'd bought in Cordova, Tennessee, about 20 miles east of downtown Memphis. That night and for the next few days, I slept with a bulletproof vest on. I slept upstairs because I thought that if someone shot my house up, they would shoot the first floor. I'd never told anyone where I lived, but Memphis is small, and I had no idea if anyone had my address.

With all the drama, I also trained myself to be able to wake up quickly and grab my gun. It's like I put myself through my own version of military training. I'd wake up early in the morning, jump up quick, and grab my gun. It seemed like I was nervous and paranoid all the time and doing whatever I could to prepare for the impending doom I felt was approaching.

Fortunately, I didn't mind being by myself. A lot of the time, I'd go to the movies by myself or drink by myself. Except when I had a woman with me, I preferred it that way.

Soon thereafter, I was told that Lord Infamous and Playa

Fly had been hanging out snorting powder. They were playing "Triple Bitch Mafia" in their car, riding around high together. Lord Infamous was crazy and wouldn't hesitate to shoot anyone, so I thought this story was wild and funny at the same time. Lord Infamous just didn't take many of the rap beefs too seriously.

Right after that, I was at the bar at a local TGI Fridays when I heard someone say, "Hey, Juicy. What's up, man?" It was Playa Fly. He was talking to me and looking at me as if nothing had ever happened between us. I had my hand on my gun and thought something was about to go down. But he was acting as if everything was cool, so I was cool.

Project Pat was ready to take things to the next level. He staked out Playa Fly's house, but I kept telling Pat that my beef with Playa Fly wasn't that serious. I told Pat that, yeah, he'd put out some songs talking shit, but that when I ran into Playa Fly, he was cool. Thankfully, I was able to convince Pat to leave Playa Fly alone.

Even with all the hype Three 6 Mafia had generated on our own, DJ Paul and I knew we needed something else to really make our mark. We had been making noise with our underground street music, but we felt we needed more money to push the group. We wanted to shoot videos, travel, and get a company vehicle. Because we had not had the big-time success we wanted, we started looking for someone to back us. We knew no bank was going to give us a loan, so we met with all the street dudes in Memphis, asking them to invest in our company. We found our investor, Nick Jackson. Also known as Nick Scarfo, he became a silent partner and helped us with our next projects, Kingpin Skinny Pimp's *King of da Playaz Ball* album and Three 6 Mafia's *The End* album, which were both released in 1996.

Things came to an end with Kingpin Skinny Pimp almost immediately. We were a small independent label just getting started and we didn't have much muscle, but *King of da Playaz Ball* was another hit for Prophet Entertainment as soon as we dropped it on March 19, 1996. Thanks to the buzz we'd built and the units we were moving independently, labels were interested in signing Skinny Pimp. He saw how people were reacting to him and thought he could do better if he was on a bigger label, like a Rap-A-Lot or a Suave House.

Since Prophet Entertainment was just getting in the game, our contract with Skinny Pimp wasn't ironclad, which he knew. DJ Paul and I didn't want Skinny Pimp to leave, but we didn't have any leverage and couldn't compete with the larger labels with deeper pockets. It would have been easy for Skinny Pimp to just leave us, so DJ Paul and I did a deal with Skinny Pimp where we bought him out of all of his rights and royalties for *King of da Playaz Ball*. Just like that, Kingpin Skinny Pimp was off of Prophet Entertainment.

Meanwhile, Playa Fly's effect on the group wasn't over. Playa Fly and Gangsta Blac were from the same neighborhood and were good friends, but we were still rolling with Gangsta Blac even after Playa Fly left the crew. We dropped Gangsta Blac's *Can It Be?* album while we were working on *The End*. Even though *Can It Be?* didn't sell much, Gangsta Blac said we owed him some money. I got the sense that he thought we weren't treating him right because of our Playa Fly beef.

That wasn't the case though, so DJ Paul and I sat down with Gangsta Blac. We reviewed his recording contract and showed him our expenses. Prophet Entertainment had genuinely spent money promoting *Can It Be?*, but he didn't understand the music business. The project hadn't recouped our initial investment, so we didn't owe Gangsta Blac any money.

Gangsta Blac's brother was cool and was trying to get us to work something out, but Gangsta Blac really seemed butthurt. He was starting to be a problem and the energy was bad, so I didn't want to work with him anymore. We bought him out of his contract, gave him some money, and he left the crew.

That's how we dealt with our artists who had issues. If we couldn't resolve the issue or things got too petty, we swallowed our pride and let them go. It was time to move on.

When I'm done with someone, I'm done with them. It didn't matter if it was business or personal. So, since Playa Fly wasn't going to sign with Prophet Entertainment, I didn't want to boost his career by dissing him. I wanted our success to kill off Playa Fly's hype, especially since he wasn't on our level anyway. Most of the beefs we had with Memphis artists were phony. Rappers would diss us just because they were jealous. There wasn't any real beef.

But the rest of the group didn't care, so we made "Gotcha Shakin'" for *The End*.

As for the rest of the album, the smooth, R&B-flavored "Late Night Tip" picked up where "Da Summa" left off. It was inspired by what dudes would say when they were going to hook up with a chick. People loved "Late Night Tip," Lord Infamous' weed anthem "Where's Da Bud," and the grisly posse cut "Body Parts." We were making different kinds of music, branching out. Three 6 Mafia was rolling, making major moves independently.

Paul and I were friends and we hung out a lot of the time, but I wasn't the type of guy to hang out with dudes a lot. I also wasn't about the negative side of things. Everybody else—DJ Paul, Lord Infamous, Gangsta Boo, Crunchy Black, and Koopsta Knicca—would get high and start fighting everybody. They'd get crazy high and pop pills, too. They'd be slurring their words. That wasn't my style.

My style was women. If anything, I had a sex addiction. I'd have three or four chicks with me. Women loved me because I was hood, but could turn it off and on. I could be clean-cut and fresh, and pull up in a car with a driver, or I could be the opposite.

In my free time, I was focused on getting with women. I wasn't really with all that extra bullshit. I don't fault anybody for it because some people like to do this and some people like to do that. So I just looked at it like, "Hey. Y'all want to get drunk, get high, and snort cocaine, shoot up a club, be my guest. Go ahead and do what you need to do. I'm not going to be there."

A good time with a good-looking woman was better in every way. Don't get me wrong, I'd ride with Three 6 Mafia to the fullest. Any time a fight broke out, I'd be the first one jumping in. If we had to go on a mission, I was in the car with them. We shot up a few things. But that wasn't really my thing. I was telling them that this wasn't the thing to do, that we needed to focus on the music. My thing was trying to stay out of trouble and be successful because I felt like we were doing something really special. We went from nothing to something, especially me.

I felt blessed to be in the situation Three 6 Mafia created. But I was never the "yes" man in the group. I was the "no" man. I was the guy who would go against everybody and wouldn't give a fuck. It didn't matter. If I didn't like your music, your song, or your verse, I wasn't going to back down. Paul used to say, "Let Juicy pick the single. He's going to keep it 100 with you." I'm not going to say I was right all the time, but I had to speak my mind.

Only having "yes" men around you is a death sentence. Anyone who is always saying, "Yeah, man. Go ahead and do it. Do that coke. Run up in the house and shoot everybody," they don't give a fuck about you. When you have somebody saying, "Nah. Don't do that drug. I wouldn't do that cocaine," that's somebody that wants to see you *alive*.

It wasn't a one-way street, though. I told everyone in the crew: "If you see me doing anything bizarre or that doesn't look right, please tell me. I'm going to listen. I'll be coming to you as a friend, a brother, somebody that actually cares about you."

That's why I was telling them not to do drugs, not to do cocaine, because I felt like it was really destroying the group. I didn't mind them smoking weed, popping pills, or downing some syrup. But every time they got on some cocaine, they would get tough and act crazy. We were still young, so our issues weren't that deep. If we were at a show and fighting backstage, all it would take was for the promoter to tell us we were going on in five minutes. Almost immediately, all the tension evaporated. Everyone was focused on giving a great performance. Still, it was just a lot for me to deal with. I wasn't trying to go to jail because of drugs or some fight that went too far. You can't make money in jail.

While the rest of the group was doing their thing, I was focused on the next steps, getting closer to the dream I had as a kid. That was definitely my main goal at the beginning stages of Prophet Entertainment and Three 6 Mafia, being the next Stax Records. I feel like I read the book *Soulsville*

U.S.A.: The Story of Stax Records 100 million times from the inside out, from the front cover to the back cover. Al Bell, the Black producer and co-owner who ran the label, had a strategy.

Stax Records was in its prime within the music business in the 1960s and 1970s. I was reading the book in the 1990s. The music business in those times was nothing like it is today, where you can access millions of songs on your phone. It's instant. When we were trying to break Three 6 Mafia and Prophet Entertainment, it was difficult to get the music, to get an album, a single. You had to go to a record store to buy it, or somebody would have to make you a copy of theirs. It took time. So yeah, somebody may have heard of an artist. Somebody may not have. At the time, Three 6 Mafia wasn't popping on a national level. We were building a buzz in Tennessee, Mississippi, Arkansas, and Georgia, but not in Florida, not in Louisiana, not in Texas.

Bell had the South, but talked about trying to break into different markets. He knew that if he could impact Chicago, they would get to the rest of the Midwest, and then New York. In the book, it details how Bell wanted to break into LA, so they did the Wattstax concert at the Coliseum in 1972. I was like, "Man. That's smart. Let me try to get some artists from other cities to help us break into those markets." So I reached out to Crucial Conflict and Twista in Chicago, Cash Money in New Orleans, Krayzie Bone in Cleveland, and Noreaga in New York. I was a fan of all these artists, but I was thinking about Al Bell's strategy. At this time, we didn't have the internet, so we actually had to go to these markets to really break into them.

Before we got big, most people had never heard many of our songs. So, we'd recycle them and bring them back because we felt like if it did well on the mixtape or one of our underground albums, it needed to be on CD, on one of our national releases so people outside of Memphis could hear it. That happened with one of our early hits. "Tear Da Club Up" was on one of DJ Paul and Lord Infamous' mixtapes. Then we redid it, added me to the song, and put it on *Mystic Stylez* in 1995. We brought it back again two years later when we got our national deal with Relativity Records.

We were doing more and more shows, but they didn't always go smoothly. We'd often have to think off the top of our heads to make sure things worked. If we did a show and Boo didn't show up, which happened all too often, I'd tell La Chat to pretend she was Boo and to perform her parts in the songs. I also told Chat that if people tried to do an interview with her to turn it down and not talk to anyone. People didn't really know what we looked like yet, so it worked.

Gangsta Boo wasn't the only one to miss shows, though. We were tired of getting burned at our concerts, so we made a show tape (the backing music we'd perform to at shows) without Koopsta Knicca, a show tape with no Lord Infamous, a show tape without Crunchy Black. DJ Paul and I also decided that we'd start doing the first verses of our songs because we knew both of us would make it to every show.

Thankfully the shows kept coming and the albums kept selling. With the success of *Mystic Stylez* and *The End*, major labels were starting to reach out to us. We flew to New York to meet with Cliff Cultreri and Alan Grunblatt from Relativity Records. The label had an incredible roster at the time, including Common, Fat Joe, The Beatnuts, Eazy-E,

MC Ren, Chi-Ali, Kokane, Dru Down, Above The Law, Bone thugs-n-harmony, M.O.P., The Dayton Family, and my old friends 8Ball & MJG.

Paul and I met Cliff and Alan at a restaurant. When they walked in, I thought they looked like Italian gangsters. They even set up the table and sat like it was a scene out of *The Godfather*. But they were big bosses at a record label. If anything, they were corporate gangsters.

What I liked about Cliff and Alan was that they didn't try to take or buy our music publishing. That was unlike every other label we'd ever spoken with. That's how the music industry was set up at the time, but I didn't like that because I thought the labels were just being greedy. They wanted to have you as an artist and your publishing, too. The industry was big on finessing artists. They didn't just try, either. They did a great job at it. I never wanted to sell my publishing, though. Even then, I was thinking that my publishing would feed me when I was old.

But at that time, the major labels wanted to own everything. One of my favorite things was that they owned the studio where they wanted you to record. Then they'd charge you to use the studio to record your songs for them. Relativity did that to us any time we'd record at Sony studios. Relativity was a Sony subsidiary.

Just like Fab 5 Freddy, Cliff and Alan flew down to Memphis. We introduced them to Lord Infamous, Gangsta Boo, Crunchy Black, and Koopsta Knicca. Everything went well, and since Relativity gave us what we wanted, we signed with them. Cliff was our A&R and main point person at the label. This was our first time having an A&R, a publicist, a national street team, and marketing people pushing us. We were now part of the machine.

The great thing about Relativity Records was that, for the most part, they let us do what we wanted to do. Paul and I handled all the music and picked all the singles. Relativity handled the promotion. It was a great arrangement.

Our single "Tear Da Club Up '97" appeared on *Chpt. 2: "World Domination,"* our first album released through the major label system. We were excited because, unlike the earlier versions of the song, all six members are featured on "Tear Da Club Up '97." Back in those days, a major label deal was the biggest thing in music. Fans around the country were finally going to get to see all of Three 6 Mafia once the song's video hit The Box, BET, and MTV. The extra muscle in the music industry with the media and retailers made you a superstar overnight. It was like being a basketball player going from college to the NBA. Whether you end up selling records or not, you have it made.

It might be difficult to imagine today, but back in 1997 Southern rap had yet to be taken seriously. Yes, Scarface, OutKast, and Goodie Mob were major acts, and Master P and UGK were exploding, but most of the music industry's attention was still focused on artists from the East Coast (Wu-Tang Clan, Busta Rhymes, Ma$e, Puff Daddy & The Family, Nas, Lil' Kim, Mobb Deep) and the West Coast (Tupac Shakur, Westside Connection, Mack 10). Artists from the South were largely dismissed, even though they had started selling millions of albums. Other than 8Ball & MJG, who had relocated to Houston, no one had broken through from Memphis, which made it harder for us to earn immediate respect but also gave us an advantage. Memphis didn't have a signature sound to the rest of the country. Because of Memphis' outsider status, I felt like an underdog, a feeling I maintained for most of my life. I always felt like people underestimated me.

Given that reality, it felt like my dreams were coming true just being able to shoot a video in Memphis. Director Marc Klasfeld captured our culture in the video for "Tear Da Club Up '97." Turning up, that's normal for us in Memphis, but I imagine someone who had never experienced that would have been shocked. They probably had never seen people with masks on and their shirts off jamming to this different type of music and doing our dances. It was so exciting to be able to show the world what Memphis was about.

Once the "Tear Da Club Up '97" video hit, I was hitting my knees every day to thank God. The blessings were coming in waves. An Atlanta-based DJ, DJ Herb, called us up out of the blue. He'd done a booty mix of "Tear Da Club Up '97." He told us it was blowing up in A-Town and that we needed to do a show there. Every time I'd been to Atlanta up to that point, the music in the clubs was all booty-shake stuff like 95 South, Luke Skyywalker, and DJ Smurf. They loved dance music.

Atlanta was full of Black people, had plenty of Black businesses, and the city looked Black-operated, too. I loved seeing Black people just chillin' and having a good time. All the people there were so cool, especially to us. Coming up in Memphis, I'd never experienced anything like that.

We went to Atlanta and performed at The Gate club. The reaction was good, but when we did "Tear Da Club Up '97," the crowd went crazy. That was one of the first times that I thought we really had something that was spreading across the country. Mississippi, Alabama, and Texas started rocking with us even more than before. I knew something bigger was happening. I thought the blessings were coming.

While we were in Atlanta, we noticed that they were playing 8Ball & MJG's underground hit "Mr. Big." After Three 6 Mafia's performance, we started noticing Atlanta was embracing more crunk songs like ours.

Without knowing it, we'd helped popularize "chant music." Some people call it "get buck music" or "crunk music." Regardless, Memphis artists happened to write their choruses in a way where they could easily be chanted by a crowd any time the record was played in a club or during a performance. 8Ball & MJG did it with "Mr. Big." I'd done it with "Don't Be Scared, Put A Rubber On The Head." Three 6 Mafia had done it with "Blow Yo Ass Off," "Tear Da Club Up," and "Get Buck Mutha Fucka," among others. We always had turnt-up fight hooks. Niggas would fight in the club, so we made fight songs.

Sometimes, things went too far. People would really tear the club up, throwing bottles and chairs, and getting into fights every time we'd perform "Tear Da Club Up." That was bad business for concert promoters and club owners, so they started putting it in our contracts that we couldn't perform "Tear Da Club Up" at our shows. We did it anyway.

Everything was exploding. We got more shows, more money, more girls. Pat was out of jail and we were all making music. The drugs had been there, but they kicked in a little harder. The hate went up, too.

After all the love we got in Atlanta, we thought about relocating there in order to get more recognition. We'd put a down payment on a house, but word about our potential move got to the owner of Cotton Row Studios in Memphis, where we recorded *Mystic Stylez*. He told us that we were about to make a big mistake. He knew we were the only people in Memphis making noise and that we could really make our name in our hometown. I'd also fallen in love with a girl in Memphis and I didn't want to leave her.

The more I thought about it, though, the more I realized the studio owner was right. If we stayed in Memphis, we'd really be on our way to achieving one of my dreams: to be like Stax Records. Atlanta already had Jermaine Dupri, LaFace Records, and other major players. Once, we even saw Jermaine Dupri standing on the street in Atlanta talking to some chicks. We pulled up on him and gave him our music. He never called us, but later he told us that he remembered the day when we gave him our CD.

"Tear Da Club Up '97" was our first major hit single, and Three 6 Mafia ended up selling more records than ever before. Relativity helped break us nationwide and we started getting write-ups in national magazines like *Rap Pages*.

Chpt. 2: "World Domination" didn't do crazy numbers right away. The sales kept increasing, though, going from 20,000 a week to 30,000 a week and then 40,000 a week. Relativity was excited as they watched the sales keep going up and up. After eight months, *Chpt. 2: "World Domination"* had sold more than 500,000 units, earning Three 6 Mafia our first gold album.

I liked going gold, but I didn't always like the overall experience of being signed to a major label. Relativity treated us like royalty, but in the back of my mind, I always felt like I was being controlled in some way. Relativity still had somewhat of a say in what we were doing, and I didn't like that.

Case in point, we were in New York one time and Gangsta Boo was acting like a real diva and running up our limousine bill. She was using a car service to go all around Manhattan shopping. I told the people at Relativity to stop letting our artist run up a bill if they were going to take it out of our check, which they were. I shouldn't have had to call someone to stop running up bills on my behalf without my knowledge.

I ended up having to cuss Alan out about that situation. To his credit, Alan ended up firing the woman who worked there and was authorizing Boo to run up those expenses. That made me feel like Alan really did have my back. Ultimately, I think that Boo finessed the employee, but whatever bill Boo ran up for personal expenses shouldn't have come out of Hypnotize Minds' pocket.

I talked to Boo about acting like this. I approached it like a daddy who was trying to speak with his daughter. She said she understood, and I'd tell her that we were going to make it, but that I needed to know what was going on. We weren't in a position to waste money, I'd tell her. We needed to use what money we had to promote our albums by running commercials and booking more studio time.

Making songs is cool, but you've got to promote them. At this point, DJ Paul and I had been selling our mixtapes out of the trunks of our cars, going to stores ourselves, and setting up our own shows for years. Nobody talks about that part, the grind. They just want to talk about the music, not the legwork and the money you've got to put up to be successful. It takes real effort to make real money. DJ Paul and I understood that from the beginning.

When people would meet us, they'd be like, "When I first heard your music, I thought y'all were devil worshippers. I thought I'd walk in the studio and see you doing a ritual with a cross or a Ouija board and I'd have to run out. Now that I've met you, y'all are actually cool, smart, and not as crazy as I thought you'd be." After people spent time with us, they walked away knowing that we were smart and serious.

Regardless of what else we had going on, Paul and I always made a point of staying on top of our business. The thing about our deal with Relativity was that they let us keep putting out projects through Select-O-Hits. With a major label like Relativity, you get an advance up front. But in order to see any royalties, you've got to sell enough units to make up the company's investment in you. With our Select-O-Hits deal, we'd see money as soon as we sold the first piece of product. We'd get a check every month from Select-O-Hits and twice a year from Relativity *if* we recouped our expenses.

With that in mind, even though we got with a major, we didn't feel like we should run all our projects through there. Alan Grunblatt at Relativity told us that he didn't care that we were still putting out independent projects.

When people saw what we were doing—putting out things on a major label through Relativity and still dropping our independent albums via Select-O-Hits—they couldn't believe it. Three 6 Mafia was the major group, so they were on the major label, Relativity. T-Rock, Killa Klan Kaze, Paul and me with our solo albums, and later La Chat, Lil Wyte and Frayser Boy, we looked at those albums as independent and extra money in our pocket. That independent money we were getting by dropping projects through Select-O-Hits was too good to give up. We were making a lot of money, a couple million here, a couple million there. Money was rolling in real fast.

When we'd be on the road, we'd be dancing on our tour bus together. Gangsta Boo would be cracking jokes. The love was there.

We were in a groove and I was trying to maximize every opportunity we had. Paul and I came to an agreement. If an album had 10 songs, he'd produce five songs and I'd produce the other five. We'd often collaborate on our songs, but we wanted it to be as equal as possible between us. We also decided to split the publishing and ownership of the songs, regardless of who made them. We wanted to do as much as we could to remove egos. Paul and I didn't want to push for a single because one of us did it. We wanted to only be concerned with picking the best songs.

I was the first one in the studio every day, usually there at 7 a.m. I was ready to go. Paul would come at 5 or 6 p.m. because he'd been up all night, and would stay until I arrived the next morning. Paul and I were often the only ones in the studio, other than the engineer and someone working the phones for us. It's not because we didn't want anyone else there with us. They just didn't show up. Other times, if I knew someone was on too many drugs, I'd just do what I had to do and leave before some of the other members would show up. I didn't want to be around all that madness. I quickly realized that I wasn't going to be hanging out a lot and kicking it with everyone.

That's why I always tried to keep things on a business level. I knew we had a good thing going and I knew we didn't have to be friends to make money. We just had to go to the studio, record some songs, do some shows, and we could each go our own way. Crunchy Black, Koopsta Knicca, and Lord Infamous would hang out. DJ Paul would hang out with Crunchy and Lord. Even though they hung out together, they'd still have tension with each other.

Crunchy was reckless. I thought he was a ticking time bomb. Sometimes he'd just pull out a gun and start shooting without even thinking. That's just how he was. A lot of the chaos he created was unnecessary. Knowing who Crunchy was before, the low-key dancer I met a few years ago, I didn't want to see that.

Thankfully, Paul and I worked well together, which kept things running smoothly. We worked Monday through Friday and took the weekends off. That was our routine, and it was working well. We'd do our own beats, and we'd work on beats together. I would sample a lot. If I wanted to play a bassline, I would riff a couple of notes and then loop it. We usually came up with the hooks and song ideas, too. We'd have a list of subjects we wanted to talk about. If we had 16 songs on an album, every song had to talk about a different subject. We'd look at our list, and we'd do a crunk song like "Tear Da Club Up," a serious song like "In-2-Deep," a weed song like "Now I'm Hi Pt. 3," a killer song like "Walk Up 2 Yo House," a robbery song like "Sweet Robbery," a song about bitches like "Porno Movie." We talked about what was going on in our neighborhood and in the streets of Memphis.

My parents didn't listen to much of my music. When my mom did happen to hear a song, she would complain about the content. My father dismissed her concerns. He was happy that I was starting to become successful and that I wasn't out there robbing anybody to get my money. He didn't care about our sometimes demonic image, either. Like me, he just took it as a gimmick.

My father was happy that I was making an honest living. It really hurt my father that Pat had gotten arrested for robbery. He knew that committing one crime usually led to committing more, to being shot at, to going back and forth to and in and out of jail. He didn't want that for his kids, so he was happy for me.

While my dad was enjoying my success from afar, my drive kept me focused. I wanted to make it so bad that I was hustling 24 hours a day. If my family wanted to see me, they'd have to come down to the studio or catch me at a show. We were on a major label, selling hundreds of thousands of albums, and performing in more and more places around the country. My dream was starting to become a reality.

Even with all this success early in the business, Three 6 Mafia wasn't a happy group. It didn't take long for me to realize that everybody in Three 6 Mafia hated each other. There was a lot of jealousy, and we'd diss each other on our own songs. Paul and I didn't care about that because if that's what it took for them to let their rage out, so be it—as long as it sounded good. Plus, they didn't name names. They were subliminal disses, maybe even just a competition thing in some cases.

But I knew what we were dealing with: Memphis is a city filled with haters, and we suffered from that. I would hear things that somebody in the group had said about me. Yeah, we'd be in the studio together. Maybe we'd go to a club. But things got to the point where I didn't want to be around them because Lord Infamous would snort some coke and he would lose his fuckin' mind. He and Paul were in a group together before I linked up with them, so Lord was upset. He wanted to be an owner of our company, too. Lord didn't think I should have had what I had since I came along after he and Paul were already making music together.

What I've heard through other members is that Lord felt

that Paul should have made him a part of our business. But Paul even told me Lord couldn't help us run the company because of his drug issues. Even though Paul has admitted to using cocaine, he was nothing like Lord Infamous, who had a *serious* drug problem. Maybe that's part of the reason why Paul and Lord used to argue all the time. A lot of stuff that was going on between them I didn't even know about. Lord never came to me and said, "Hey, man. I don't like how this is going. I think I should be this and that."

One day we were all in the car about to do a show. We were all talking and all of a sudden Lord was like, "Ahhhh. Fuck you, Paul!" He jumped on Paul, and I had to pull Lord off him. They got out of the car and started fighting.

At the beginning of our relationship, it seemed like Paul and Lord had a genuine love for one another. But as Three 6 Mafia got more and more successful, it felt like they hated each other more and more.

It seemed like Lord was always mad, and it was the same with some of the other members of the group. The cocaine really changed them. One minute they'd be cool. Then they'd hit some cocaine and the next minute, they'd want to fight everybody. The Devil would come out. Guns would get pulled on a regular basis and they'd want to shoot up everything. They were straight maniacs.

On top of that, everybody wasn't getting the same amount of money because everybody wasn't doing what Paul and I were doing. That led to a lot of jealousy. Everybody had egos. I had one. Everybody thought they were the shit and had their own way that they wanted to do things. Even if somebody rapped better than me in the group, I didn't care. I still thought I was better than them.

But I never let my ego make it like I was trying to leave

the group. I would try to keep the group together. But there was a lot of tension going on. Something between Paul and Boo always led to a fight. Maybe she liked Paul. I don't know. But Boo was on the cocaine and Crunchy was going wild. It seemed like every fuckin' week, Crunchy Black was shooting at somebody, fighting somebody. Something very bad was always going down.

One time, some guys had done some stuff to Crunchy. I had to pull a gun on them so they'd get out of Dodge. That's when I started hiring security. Things were getting serious in the streets. I had money at that point, so I figured I'd pay someone to shoot someone if I had to.

It seemed like Crunchy always ended up in some sort of trouble. I bailed him out of jail so many times that I lost count. I'd talk to him, try to get him off drugs and try to calm him down. I wanted the best for Crunchy, but we still had to do our business, which was Three 6 Mafia and making music.

Things were spiraling out of control. Sometimes we'd have what seemed like 100 people at the studio. I was recording my verse to "Tear Da Club Up '97" and somebody hollered out, "Nah, man. Don't say it like that. Say it like this."

"Who the fuck just said that?" I roared.

I looked at Paul. "If I mess up or need to change something, *you* talk to me," I told him and everyone else. "Nobody else say shit to me. You're the producer. I'm the producer. We do the production."

On top of that, the guy who owned the studio told me that somebody had stolen his checkbook. And sometimes my friend Big Triece would be passed out in the front of the studio, and we'd have to step over his big ass to even get

CHRONICLES OF THE JUICE MAN

into the building. People would be fighting in the middle of recording sessions.

I knew this environment wasn't helpful for getting work done, so I shut the studio down to outsiders. I hung a sign up on the door to our studio: "No Dope Dealers. No Bank Robbers. No Phones. No Sisters. No Friends."

The rest of the group hated me for that, but I didn't want anything to bring us down. We were running a business and that's how I treated it. I didn't allow guns in the studio. I also started fining people if they were late to the studio, which had become an issue. Regardless of how they felt about it, everyone in Three 6 Mafia knew they were in good hands with me handling things. My goal was to keep things professional and organized, and my only driving motivation was what was best for the group.

Crunchy had been in and out of jail between *Mystic Stylez* in 1995 and when we released *Chpt. 2: "World Domination"* in 1997. I felt like we had a great opportunity to make money, be famous, and do everything we wanted to do in life, but we had people in the crew fucking it up. To be from Memphis and making money from rap was unheard of. Too much was at stake, so one day DJ Paul and I said, "New rules. We ain't getting nobody out of jail. You go to jail, you stay in jail."

Despite all the problems, we really were down for each other. We were doing a photo shoot for *XXL* magazine. The photographer had a big truck with a bunch of lights, cameras, and other equipment. After he parked, he met us on a hill. We were location scouting, so he left his gear in the truck. As we were looking around, some dudes pulled up, saw the equipment in the truck, grabbed it, put it in their trunk, and took off. Crunchy told us he saw them

JUICY J AND SOREN BAKER

drive off, so we jumped in my car. We drove around downtown Memphis looking for them. We finally saw them heading the other direction, so I swerved around and cut them off. We were yelling at them, "Yo. Where's the shit at?!?" They acted like they didn't know what we were talking about. I knew they were lying, so I pulled my chrome Smith & Wesson .357 out and aimed it at them. "Stop playin'," I said.

Dude said, "It's in the trunk."

Crunchy and I got out of the car and the dudes were scared as hell. They put their hands on the dash. Crunchy grabbed the stuff out of the trunk, put it in the back of my car, and we drove off. As I pulled off, I looked in my rearview mirror and saw a White guy on the phone. Fortunately, nothing came of it.

Koopsta, though, was continuing his descent. In the early days, he was a team player and was giving his all to Three 6 Mafia. Eventually that was gone, though. He was snorting so much cocaine and always acting a damn fool. Koop would go to jail for months and would almost never show up at the studio. When he did show up, DJ Paul and I would put him last on the songs. We figured that if we ended up doing that song at a show, it'd be easier to cut his verse out of the performance if he missed the show.

Lots of people told us that he'd be locked up and talking shit about the group. Plus, he'd miss photo shoots, which is why he wasn't on a lot of our album covers. He'd become the weakest link in the group.

Sometimes, Koopsta would be homeless. Other times, he'd stay with DJ Paul. He was destructive and would do anything. If you asked him to rob a bank, he'd do it. He'd get girls pregnant and wouldn't care. He'd even talk about

128

street shit we did. From my perspective, that was disloyal. We'd gotten this man out of jail, put food on his table, made sure he was paid, and tried to take him to rehab so many times. Crunchy Black was turnt up, but Koopsta Knicca was *crazy*. He wasn't smart.

I remember buying Koop a brand-new car even though he had plenty of money in his pocket. Some people found him passed out in his car in a ditch somewhere in Memphis. He'd been high and literally run into a ditch.

Another time I wrote a check to Koop. He said he lost it, but he had already cashed it and just came back trying to get another one. Koop was ratchet like that. I couldn't trust him.

I'd be in the studio with a gun on me at all times because I didn't know what was going to happen.

As if all this drama wasn't enough, our silent partner, Nick Jackson, started changing, too. He'd gone to jail, paid his debt to society. We were blowing up when he got out of jail. Then he went to jail again, but he got right back out. But I didn't really care because he was just a private investor in our company. He was getting checks from us.

Then all of a sudden, Nick wanted to be front and center in the operation. He didn't want to just back us anymore. He wanted to rap, be on the album covers, and get a piece of the publishing even though he wasn't writing any of the songs and hadn't even been in the studio. He wanted to get a third of everything, including our money from shows. He wanted to come to the studio and bring all his niggas from the hood. He wanted to have groups on the label and, really, run the company, even though he only owned a third of it at that point. Paul and I told him no. We had all agreed that he'd be a backer, a silent partner. We didn't want anyone we didn't know at the studio.

On top of that, Nick started snorting powder. He'd lost focus on our initial vision and the cocaine had turned him into a monster. Like most people on coke, when he'd be coming down off his high, he was crazy and angry. It really fucked him up.

We couldn't agree on how our partnership would continue, so Nick sued us. Paul and I eventually ended up buying Nick out. Nick got the name Prophet Entertainment, our Teflon Music publishing company, and $400,000. Paul paid $200,000 and as I was writing my $200,000 check, I thought, "Man. This nigga isn't thinking long-range. He's about to get a lot of money, but he doesn't understand what he's about to lose."

I looked at it like we got rid of a headache. I was happy to give Nick that $400,000. Since we didn't have Prophet Entertainment anymore, Paul and I launched Tefnoise Music for our music publishing and made Hypnotize Minds Productions our new label. We used the latter for both our Select-O-Hits releases and our Relativity Records projects.

Paul and I liked Hypnotize Minds because it had a mystical and magical vibe. We felt like our music was really hypnotizing people's minds, getting them to tear the club up and do crazy shit. That's why the name worked.

After we did the deal and went our separate ways, Nick came back and said he needed more money. That wasn't going to happen, but I imagined that he'd thought about what he'd done. He'd probably realized that he had walked away from hundreds of millions of dollars, big success, and opportunity. We went back to court and the judge ruled that he couldn't just change his mind. The judge ruled in our favor because the deal was done fairly and properly.

That's when Nick started dissing us, throwing parties, and saying that he'd sued us. He'd gotten everything he'd said he wanted in order to be bought out, but he was still mad. I felt like he was hurt because he'd lost one of the biggest groups in music. All he had to do was sit back and chill and he would have been with us for the long run. If he would have just kept his mouth shut and played his part as a silent partner, he would have been twice as rich. Not everybody thinks like that, though. They want it all now. But he got his money and that was it. (Nick passed away in August 2015. RIP.)

Other problems were mounting, too. It seemed like death was around the corner—either for me or someone else in Three 6 Mafia.

CHAPTER

7

BIG BIZNESS

AFTER THE SUCCESS OF *Chpt. 2: "World Domination,"* we had no intentions of slowing down. Debut solo albums from Indo G and Gangsta Boo were up next. But as I'd seen with the limo situation, Boo was hard to deal with. Nonetheless, she was just so good at rapping.

When we'd perform, she'd sit in the corner waiting for her verse to come on. When it did, she'd jump up, start rapping, and the crowd would go crazy. That got to her head and she wanted everything. If Lil' Kim had something, she wanted it, too. DJ Paul and I didn't want her to be all glamorous like Lil' Kim. After all, Boo had started off calling herself "The Devil's Daughter." I had to tell her to chill out, but she would come to the studio and talk shit to Paul and me. Boo wanted to be a boss, but DJ Paul and I were the only bosses.

Indo G's *Angel Dust* album arrived August 25, 1998, and

didn't sell much, so we mutually decided to part ways soon thereafter. *Enquiring Minds* arrived in stores a month later. While it did better than *Angel Dust*, *Enquiring Minds* didn't break out. It was cool, but I thought the album could have been better. Boo's flow had changed, and I didn't like it. Her ego had gotten so big, and she was very upset. People liked the single "Where Dem Dollas At," but the rest of the album didn't make much noise.

I was really trying to keep everyone in line so that we could all succeed and get paid. They were all wild, though.

Koopsta was in jail *all the time*, even more than Crunchy Black. Paul and Koopsta had gotten into a fight at one of our parties. Our album had just gone gold and they were fighting. Everybody was in there drunk, and on drugs. In the midst of the argument, Paul told Koopsta that he wasn't in Three 6 Mafia anymore. When Paul kicked him out of the group, I was like, "Good." I just felt like he was a problem. The public didn't know Koop was gone. We kept our group business in-house. Soon thereafter, we let him back into the group and he'd say foul shit about us behind our backs.

Another time, we were at a concert in Atlanta around 1998 or so and I was talking to Master P about putting out independent music. P was upset because one of the companies he was working with owed him hundreds of millions of dollars. "I don't hang around no fake niggas. No rats," Master P said right before he stormed out of the dressing room with his entourage.

As soon as P said that, I started thinking about Koopsta Knicca. I felt he'd dissed us, the people that really had his back. To me, he was a traitor, especially after all that DJ Paul and I had done for him. We'd put him in rehab, gotten him out of jail numerous times, and gone on street missions with him.

I was like, "Paul, you hear that? He's right. I don't want to hang around any fake motherfuckas, like this dude here." Koopsta had been sitting on the couch, but when he realized I was talking about him, he stood up. As soon as Koopsta got up, I hit him in the face. Then Project Pat pulled out a gun.

"This ain't what y'all want." Pat was right, so I ended up fighting Koopsta and beating the brakes off of him. I put all my anger into every punch, stomp, and hit. I was so mad at him that I couldn't take it anymore.

When we ended up on the tour bus later that night, Lord Infamous was mad at Paul. Lord didn't like that Paul had let me fight Koop. In front of everybody, Paul said, "Shoot that muthafucka." One of our security guards at the time—we called him Medicine Man because he was taking "medicine," but it was really just Xanax and stuff he'd buy on the street—raised his strap. Medicine Man was about to shoot Koop, so I grabbed his hand and told him to put the gun down. "I'm just doing my job," he told me. Medicine Man gave me the gun. I just wanted to whoop Koop's ass, not see him die.

Lord Infamous was pissed and got off the bus. Boo was mad, too, and left with someone else. Everyone had calmed down, so everyone in the group other than Boo got back on the bus headed back to Memphis. No one talked to Koop on the ride home.

Right after that, Koopsta came to the studio to pick up a check. I had a TEC-9 at the time and told Paul that if Koop came up to see us that I was going to shoot him. I told Paul to go talk to Koop and let him know that we'd mail him his check. That was it with Koopsta Knicca. I was done with him. It was time to move on and focus on other things.

We were done with Koopsta, but he wasn't finished with us. After we kicked him out of the group, he got a lawyer and had us tied up in litigation for about a year. Even with all that, DJ Paul and I still took care of Koopsta and made sure he was paid. We bought him out of everything, all of his royalties and publishing. Koop wanted to be done with us, so buying him out was a small price to pay. I was so glad he was gone, that we didn't have to deal with that level of ignorance anymore. (In 1999, DJ Paul did a deal that didn't involve me with Select-O-Hits to release Koopsta's *Da Devil's Playground: Underground Solo* as an album.)

I felt like Otis Williams from The Temptations, the senior group member who kept everything and everyone in line. Group members could come and go, but nobody was going to stop the show. Three 6 Mafia was down to five members: DJ Paul, Lord Infamous, Gangsta Boo, Crunchy Black, and me.

Later that year, DJ Paul, Lord Infamous, and I were working on our side group called Tear Da Club Up Thugs. The three of us had started Triple Six Mafia, so this album was a sort of tribute to us as founders of the group. We also wanted some big features, so we put Too $hort, Twista, Cash Money, and others on the record.

I decided to remake "Slob On My Nob" for the album because it was still hot in the streets. When you listen to the version I put out on my mixtapes, it didn't have any music on it. It was just a drumbeat. I had put a piano on the second version, but I wanted to spice it up a bit. I redid it and put it back out. We were starting to get some national buzz, but "Slob On My Nob" had never gotten played on the radio. It was an underground hit, and every time I'd perform it, people would go crazy. So I decided to put it on the Tear Da Club Up Thugs album, *CrazyNDaLaz-Dayz*, which arrived in stores February 2, 1999. Being on that album took "Slob On My Nob" to another level. It was finally put out on a major label and the song spread everywhere. The song had been out for four or five years to that point. Today, the song has more than 50 million streams on Spotify.

Every month, we were getting more integrated into the Relativity Records system. We weren't getting too much radio play, but we had the underground and the hood clubs on lock.

I wanted to build on our momentum, so I took my grind to another level. I was up early at the studio every day, eager to get on the phone and talk to people at Relativity about marketing, discuss radio, and go over the charts. I wanted to let the label know that they weren't alone. We were investing in our career and putting our own money up to make things happen. We even used some of our advance money for promotion.

Since we had also been earning more money from our independent releases and getting budgets from Relativity, Paul and I were investing in better equipment. In the mixtape days, we'd been using the SP-1200 and the Roland W-30 keyboard on almost every song. Then we got an Ensoniq ASR-10 keyboard, which featured 62 effects, including a vocoder and distortion. The ASR-10 also allowed us to modify, stack, and manipulate sounds in a variety of new and different ways. We also started experimenting more with live musicians to make our sound bigger, while still keeping the Three 6 Mafia vibes.

Our sound was evolving. With these new resources at Paul's and my disposal, our production improved dramatically.

By this time, Project Pat was out of prison and seeing the money we were making. He wanted in. I'd produced his first mixtape, *Murderers & Robbers*. The tape was real raw. Now Three 6 Mafia talked about street stuff, but we were also tearing the club up, getting buck. Pat wasn't talking about that. His vibe was street shit. Pat wanted people to know that he was a street person. A *real* street person. I couldn't understand it. I told him that he didn't have anything to prove to anyone. He wanted to put his albums out and still be on the same street corners. But he was smart and knew how to put words together.

We'd reintroduced Pat to the game by teaming him with Scan Man and M.C. Mack. As a trio, they were The Kaze, aka Killa Klan Kaze. We dropped their *Kamakazie Timez Up* LP in September 1998. Songs such as "Hard Not To Kill" and "Niggas Got Me Fucked Up" were hot locally as we began working on Pat's debut solo album, which we would release through Hypnotize Minds in conjunction with Relativity Records.

Project Pat started his *Ghetty Green* album with the song "North Memphis." Then he had "Represent It" with Noreaga, basically saying "if you're in the street, represent it."

"Out There" was one of my favorite songs because that's Memphis slang for saying "you're out there in these streets." He was rapping about being *"Fourth floor bound, mane/That's if I get caught, mane."* The fourth floor is the worst part of the jail he went to the first time he got locked up. They could kill you, shank you, beat the fuck out of you. Anything could happen on that fourth floor.

Anything could happen in the studio, too. We were bringing in guitar players, horn players, violinists, piano players, opera singers. Whatever it would take to make our songs better, we'd try it. We knew a guy who said his girl would let him fuck her in the recording booth, so for the *Ghetty Green* song "Run A Train," we mic'd the booth up and recorded them having sex. They were doing it the whole time Pat was rapping. So when you hear the girl getting smacked on her ass, she was really getting smacked on the ass. Our engineer was getting head, too.

Project Pat was so street that we felt he could really reach the hoods in other cities. We decided to connect him with street rappers from around the country, like New York's Noreaga, Cleveland's Krayzie Bone, and Chicago's Crucial Conflict. We'd been doing songs with Cash Money Records artists for years, so that was a natural fit, too. We liked the music of everyone we asked to get on Pat's album. That was the main thing.

We were in the studio recording "Ballers" with Juvenile, The Big Tymers, and the Hot Boyz. I kept telling Pat that that was his style. He didn't know what I was talking about. At the beginning of his verse, he said, *"Jumping off the trizzack/Chiefing on a sizacc/Sippin' on some sizurp."* I told him to use that style, not on every song, but here and there. I told him that was going to be his shit. I told him when people would hear his voice and melody, they'd be like, "Oh. That's Project Pat." It would make him stick out.

Project Pat brought that extra element that our crew needed, that strength. *Ghetty Green* was a dope album, real raw, and had a lot of great collaborations. It dropped September 14, 1999, and it made people realize that we for real. Hypnotize Minds now had a legitimate roster.

I wanted to do legit things for my family, too, but the ghosts of past experiences were hard to shake. Money was rolling in and I wanted to take care of my mom, but her experience growing up as a Black woman in Memphis had a big effect on her psyche. When I bought her a house on the outskirts of Memphis in a real nice neighborhood, the first thing she told me was, "I don't know. I don't know about moving out there." I was trying to get her out of the hood, so I asked her why. She said, "Them White folks out there..." and she trailed off.

"Mama," I told her, "we're not living in the '60s anymore."

My mom came from the era of the colored bathrooms and segregated schools. My mom had experienced people throwing stuff at her and trying to fight her—not because she stole anything or did something wrong—just because she was Black. Even though things weren't like that anymore, I felt like she was trapped in those days.

I knew racism was still alive, but I stressed to my mom that it wasn't like when she grew up, that it was safe for us to live in these places. I knew and worked with several nice White people and was doing great business with Select-O-Hits, and they were White. I was raised to judge people by their character, not their color. None of that mattered to my mom. Her wounds were too deep. It took her an entire year before she moved into that house.

With all that was happening, I felt like I had a demon side of me, that I was really crazy. But I had another side of me that was thinking straight and saying, "Nah. We're not doing that."

"If we go shoot up this house and somebody gets shot in the head, that person you're with, that you paid $25 to shoot up this house, do you think they're going to snitch on you if you get caught?"

"Are these people you're with really gangsters? Do you really think they're about this kind of life?"

"This street code that you say you live by, is it really real? Or is it just something somebody else made up? Is it a myth, a fairy tale?"

I felt like I had a split personality, a "Fuck it" side and a "Fear" side. It was a real fight to control my mind. The war going on in my mind saved my life. I knew I had too much to lose to keep doing dumb shit in the streets.

Sometimes, my internal battle got so bad that I would cry myself to sleep at night. I was truly at war within myself. On top of that, living in Memphis, I was finding it increasingly difficult to know who to trust. I knew so many people who'd gotten double-crossed and set up. Fortunately, I had music.

We had mostly a Black fan base until the year 2000. By that point, we'd helped create a dope-ass wave with our chant music that had lasted several years. I felt like we'd conquered that and wanted to try to do some different things musically. We had other records in us that I felt people would mess with just like they did with "Tear Da Club Up."

The music business goes through constant changes, and after successful releases from Three 6 Mafia, Project Pat, Gangsta Boo, and Tear Da Club Up Thugs, Relativity Records was merged into Loud Records. The label was owned by Steve Rifkind, a promotions expert who launched Loud and had enjoyed tremendous success with Wu-Tang Clan, Mobb Deep, and Raekwon.

When Relativity was absorbed by Loud, we lost Cliff Cultreri and Alan Grunblatt, as well as our publicist Grace Heck and other people who really had our back and had helped Three 6 Mafia break through. I had real, genuine love for the people at Relativity because they believed in our music and they didn't stand in our way. If we didn't want them to come to the studio, they didn't come. If we wanted to market ourselves in a certain way, they supported us.

Relativity would have people in the streets promoting us and would introduce us to their contacts at different radio stations across the country. They liked what we were doing and encouraged us to keep going. Looking back, that was the best team of people I ever worked with in the major label system, and Cliff and Alan were my favorites.

Being at Loud was a different experience. I liked that Loud had more of a hood vibe and that you could smoke weed in their office. Steve Rifkind was cool and would give us what we wanted, but other people would come in and start telling us what to do. Steve's partner, Rich Isaacson, in particular, would try to undo whatever Steve had promised us. I didn't know what to make of their relationship. I'd never seen two executives clash like that.

Even though we worked virtually nonstop, we never rushed anything. That's why our music sounded different on each album, and each artist had their own vibe. As our career progressed, Three 6 Mafia albums became bigger and bigger deals. Those albums were events, with a bunch of different voices, characters, personalities, and vibes.

Paul and I would really have to concentrate to make Three 6 Mafia albums special. That's why there was a two-and-a-half-year gap between *Chpt. 2: "World Domination"* and its follow-up, *When The Smoke Clears: Sixty 6, Sixty 1.* We wanted to make sure every Three 6 Mafia album was a classic.

We also felt that people had started copying and co-opting our sound. It didn't bother me much, though. If you're good at what you do, like Prince or Willie Hutch, people are going to want to be like you. That's why we sampled who we sampled. We liked what they were doing.

Since people had taken our crunk sound, DJ Paul and I decided to try something else and come up with some-thing different. I loved doing that and would always push Paul to do the same. We didn't go into the studio trying to manufacture a hit, but we ended up making "Sippin' On Some Syrup" and a bunch of other material for Three 6 Mafia's next album.

I took a line from Project Pat's "Ballers" and used that as the chorus for "Sippin' On Some Syrup." The reason why DJ Paul and I are the only Three 6 Mafia members on the song was because nobody else showed up to the studio, not Lord Infamous, not Gangsta Boo, not Crunchy Black. All three of them were supposed to be on "Sippin' On Some Syrup," but they weren't answering their phones. That's why Paul and I decided to put Pimp C and Bun B on it. We'd known them for years, so it was a perfect opportu-nity to collaborate.

After Paul and I did our verses, we drove down to At-lanta and almost killed ourselves in the process. It was Jan-uary 2000 and we didn't know it, but Atlanta was in the midst of a massive ice storm that left half a million customers without power. As we were driving down there, a car started coming at us, spinning out of control from the opposite side of the road. Paul and I jumped out and ran away from our car.

Once things were clear, we got back in the car and drove to Pimp C's house. He lived on this big hill, and cars were sliding everywhere. We actually had to hold each other's hands and pull each other up to get to his house. There was so much ice. That night, though, we recorded "Sippin' On Some Syrup," and we were glad we didn't wait around for Lord Infamous, Gangsta Boo, and Crunchy Black to show up.

From that point on, if someone didn't show up to the studio, they weren't going to be on the song. We weren't waiting around.

Excited to share our new material with the people at Loud, DJ Paul and I had a meeting with Steve Rifkind in New York. We brought "Sippin' On Some Syrup" and two other songs, not thinking that "Sippin' On Some Syrup" would be a single. We thought a different song with Pimp C was the one. Steve Rifkind liked "Sippin' On Some Syrup." So did the rest of his staff. DJ Paul and I weren't so sure. We were riding hard for the other song with Pimp C.

I was nervous because "Sippin' On Some Syrup" was so different for us. It was slow. Yes, it had Pimp C and Bun B on it, but it wasn't the usual "Tear Da Club Up" type of song our fans loved us for. But I knew we couldn't do only crunk songs and that we needed to change things up in order to keep our fans guessing. After putting a lot of work in on the album, "Sippin' On Some Syrup" was my favorite song we recorded for *When The Smoke Clears: Sixty 6, Sixty 1*—and everyone was telling me it was a hit.

I had cautious optimism about how people would react to "Sippin' On Some Syrup" because everyone that heard it loved it, but I also had a policy of not getting too hyped up about something before it happened. I didn't want to invest too much energy and emotion into something. Still, everyone at the label was hyped up for the song, so we shot a video for it.

Soon after that, Three 6 Mafia went to a mixtape summit in Nashville. Loud Records had hooked it up to where the video for "Sippin' On Some Syrup" was playing in everyone's hotel room. The song wasn't even out yet, so this was a perfect promotional tool. The song and video generated a strong buzz that weekend.

DJ Paul and some dude got into a fight, so we didn't end up performing at the event. Gangsta Boo ended up staying, but we got kicked out of the hotel and left the event early. I wanted to make sure we avoided any real problems or retaliation for Paul and the crew beating some dude's ass.

Loud Records was disappointed we didn't get to perform in front of a room full of DJs, but the mission had been accomplished. All the DJs were singing "Sippin' On Some Syrup" and the song hadn't even been released. We had a hit, the label told us.

When Loud Records released "Sippin' On Some Syrup" in February 2000, it instantly became the most popular song of our career. As soon as the song took off, Lord Infamous, Gangsta Boo, and Crunchy Black were all like, "Man. We should have come to the studio." They should have, but DJ Paul and I had known better than to wait around. "Sippin' On Some Syrup" peaked at No. 30 on the Hot R&B/ Hip-Hop Songs chart.

Loud Records was working behind the scenes to make

the song even bigger. Charlene Thomas, who worked for Loud Records and executive produced *When The Smoke Clears: Sixty 6, Sixty 1* on the Loud Records side, asked JAY-Z to get on the remix for the song. He said he liked it, but that he didn't sip syrup so he wouldn't do it.

Then Charlene took the song to Eminem. He liked "Sippin' On Some Syrup," too, but he wanted to know why Three 6 Mafia had done the song "Just Anotha Crazy Click" with his archrivals Insane Clown Posse (ICP) for *When The Smoke Clears: Sixty 6, Sixty 1*. Because we'd worked with ICP, Eminem refused to collaborate with us. Thankfully, "Sippin' On Some Syrup" had so much momentum that these remixes that never happened didn't impact our rollout.

One of the great things about Three 6 Mafia's music is that no label ever had to do much to promote our material. It really sold itself. "Sippin' On Some Syrup" was yet another example. Our lawyers would often say to us, "You guys make these labels money. They don't spend much on you, so they're making straight money."

"Sippin' On Some Syrup" helped our *When The Smoke Clears: Sixty 6, Sixty 1* album go platinum, with sales of more than 1 million copies. That's when things started changing. When you have a song that charts and is a national hit, White people start going to your shows. Sure, "Sippin' On Some Syrup" was catchy, but it was also a song about a drug so many people were doing at the time. Syrup had gotten big in Texas, which is why we put Bun B and Pimp C on the song.

It seemed like overnight we had developed a White fan base. I was shocked to see White people in the club. I didn't know that they listened to our music. We had been in small hood spots, the shoot-'em-up-bang-bang type of clubs, for so long. It was all Black folks when we'd be performing "Tear Da Club Up" or "Hit A Muthafucka." You'd see Black folks in a mosh pit, niggas with their shirts off fighting. They don't do that now. But they did for us.

Pimp C would tell us that a lot of people snort cocaine and smoke weed, but they don't talk about it in their songs. We did. It's the same with the gangster music we made. N.W.A was gangster, but we'd talk about walking up to your house, knocking on your door, and blowing your head off. We did things different.

While some crews were blowing money, Three 6 Mafia was trying to save it. When Project Pat's "Chickenhead" single featuring La Chat started taking off in late 2000 and early 2001, we were invited to perform the song on *The Jenny Jones Show* in Chicago. After running the numbers, we saw that it would be much cheaper to drive to Chi-Town than to fly there. So Project Pat, DJ Paul, La Chat (Pat wanted her on the song because he thought her grit worked well with the song's vibe), and I got in a van and drove to Chicago.

We did that for purely cost-saving reasons, but things changed once the terrorist attacks of September 11 took place. The group was supposed to be in New York a day or two after the attacks, but we decided we weren't going to be flying anywhere for the foreseeable future. For the next few years, we drove everywhere we needed to be, whether it was New York, Florida, or California.

Some people would have dreaded those long drives. We treated it like a party. We'd be drinking and having fun.

Back in Memphis, I put all of my energy into Project Pat's second major label album, *Mista Don't Play: Everythangs*

Workin. After the success of *When The Smoke Clears: Sixty 6, Sixty 1,* I knew it was going to go. The beats and rhymes worked perfectly together on that album. Pat's stories were amazing and everything just hit right. We had a special moment making *Mista Don't Play: Everythangs Workin.* It was magical.

The whole Hypnotize Minds crew was gearing up for the release of *Mista Don't Play,* but Pat couldn't leave the streets alone. He was behind an apartment building shooting pistols in the air with some of his friends. When I heard about it, I was pissed and called him immediately.

"While you're riding around and in these neighborhoods thinking you've got to prove something…" I said before he cut me off.

"Well, I'm Project Pat," he said. "Muthafuckas hear me rap about this shit. I've got to let them know what it is."

"You don't owe those muthafuckas shit," I responded. "You're stupid as fuck for doing that shit. You're going to end up calling me from jail and I'm going to be like, 'I told you so.'"

Unfortunately, that's what happened. Soon after that, Pat was driving through the hood and got pulled over. When the police searched his vehicle, they found firearms, which, as a convicted felon, was a violation of his parole. Right as his career was about to really take off, Project Pat was headed back to jail.

I'd been telling Pat to stay out of the hood, but he wouldn't listen. I was so fuckin' mad. We were right at the finish line. We were *at the door,* about to break through.

When Project Pat called me from jail, he was like, "Man, you were right."

"You know we just lost half a million dollars, right?"

I asked him. "I had shows lined up, a tour coming up. 'Chickenhead' is going crazy and your ass is locked up."

I tried my best to get him out of jail. I threw all kinds of money at the case, talking to this lawyer and that lawyer, anybody I thought could help. I was reaching out to politicians, but nothing worked.

One of Project Pat's cases was initially tried in Memphis. He won that one. The legal powers-that-be thought that the jury was prejudiced because Pat had such a huge fan base. Because of that, they moved the other trial to Jackson, Tennessee, which is about 85 miles northeast of Memphis. This time, the jury was full of people who didn't know who Pat was. This time, he was found guilty and sentenced to more than four years in prison for violating his parole and for two counts of possessing a firearm as a felon.

Unlike most companies that promote when a rapper gets locked up, Hypnotize Minds kept Pat's incarceration on the low. We didn't want to dampen the anticipation for *Mista Don't Play: Everythangs Workin*, which was set to do big numbers, so Loud Records kept promoting the album. Since Pat wasn't going to be able to be in any more videos, we found a look-alike and used him as a stand-in for Pat for the "Don't Save Her" video. Things were rolling for Pat and the camp.

While Project Pat was serving time, Hypnotize Minds was working on Gangsta Boo's second album, *Both Worlds, *69*. It was difficult making that project. She thought that DJ Paul and I would make the beats, write the hooks, and that she'd just show up and rap.

While we were working on it, she was frequently rapping like Tupac. On other songs, she was trying to be like Silkk The Shocker and rap all offbeat. I didn't like that. I felt like she was paying attention to what everybody else was doing and not being the Gangsta Boo that people knew and loved from *Mystic Stylez* to *Chpt. 2: "World Domination."* I told her that she had her own shit and that she just needed to do that. Be Gangsta Boo.

Boo's attitude was so nonchalant that I was becoming distant, slowly removing myself from her material. I'd given her everything I had on *Enquiring Minds*, but since her attitude had only worsened, I was over working with her.

I remember being in our studio and telling everyone that Project Pat was going to do 150,000 units the first week with *Mista Don't Play: Everythangs Workin*. Everyone was excited, other than Boo.

She was sitting on the couch and was not in a celebratory mood. "That ain't shit. I'ma do way more than him."

"Why are you talking like that?" I asked her. "We're a group. We're working together. We're a team. You should be happy for Pat. His success is your success, just like your success is his success. Everybody is going to capitalize off of this. You need to record with Pat. He could write you some dope-ass hooks."

Boo would always be in our faces, telling the group that she was the reason Three 6 Mafia was selling records, that she was the one fans wanted to see at shows, that she is why we had money. She was a superstar, but she had a real crazy ego and it was only getting worse.

As we were gearing up for Boo's project, a new voice was emerging. Lil Jon & The East Side Boyz had been making songs and albums for years. In 2001, the Atlanta trio broke through nationally with their *Put Yo Hood Up* album, which dropped May 22, 2001. The raucous title track and the single "Bia' Bia'" featuring Ludacris, Too $hort, Big

Kap, and Chyna Whyte were in heavy video and radio rotation, especially throughout the South. Three 6 Mafia also appeared on the album with the song "Move Bitch." The song's chorus is very similar to the famous Ludacris song with the same name that came out later that year.

Lil Jon & The East Side Boyz put their own twist on crunk music and people were loving it. The same couldn't be said for Gangsta Boo's second album. When *Both Worlds, *69* dropped July 31, 2001, it got good reviews, but it only sold about 42,000 copies the first week. She was mad as a muthafucka. Hypnotize Minds had been on a roll with Three 6 Mafia's *When The Smoke Clears: Sixty 6, Sixty 1*, which had gone platinum, and Project Pat's *Mista Don't Play: Everythangs Workin*, which had gone gold while he was locked up.

I'd pull Boo to the side and tell her that she needed to calm her lil' wild ass down, that everything would work itself out and to not worry about the slow sales. Things happen. Boo wasn't hearing it. She tried to say that she was a born-again Christian to get out of her contract with us. I laughed at the thought of Gangsta Boo going gospel. I told her that we'd given her advance money, that we had paid for her studio time, and that she needed to honor her contract and remain signed to Hypnotize Minds.

Although Boo was a key piece of Three 6 Mafia, she wasn't the main piece. Gradually, Paul and I realized that we didn't need Gangsta Boo, that she was more trouble than she was worth. We had tried to work with her, but if she didn't want to work with us, we still had La Chat.

Finally, it got to the point where Gangsta Boo's head was so big and things had gotten too stressful. I don't underestimate anybody, so I always made sure to be strapped when she came around during these times. She is Gangsta Boo for a reason. I come from the streets, so I looked at everybody as a potential monster. I wasn't looking to be surprised and find out that someone was *really* crazy and down for whatever.

I knew things were too far gone. We just had to let go. We gave her her wish, even though she was in breach of her contract. I felt like Three 6 Mafia was still going to shine regardless.

In fact, in the back of my mind, I was happy that Project Pat had picked La Chat to be on "Chickenhead." I wanted to show Boo that we didn't need her, that we could produce anything, whether she was on the song or not. With or without her, we were producing records, making albums, doing the marketing, shooting videos. DJ Paul and I would give our artists the whole package. It was our vision, our direction. It wasn't just a beat.

As was the case with Koopsta Knicca and Nick Jackson, the money was straight with Boo. Everything was being taken care of, even though she had accused Paul and me of stealing her money. (Later she apologized and admitted that she'd been paid properly. She even laughed about it.)

If Boo would have just chilled and followed our lead, everything would have been fine. The formula was working, but Boo was fucking it up and I couldn't trust her anymore. She wasn't happy being in her lane. She wanted to be like Lil' Kim and it wasn't working. Boo just wouldn't listen, so she had to go.

Even though she was in breach of her contract, Boo signed with Jacob York and his Yorktown Music. York had worked with Biggie and Lil' Kim, so maybe Boo thought he could help her get to Lil' Kim status. But he wasn't able to create a similar excitement with Boo, either, and she soon severed business ties with York, too.

I really wish Boo could have let her ego go and would have come back to us. But she never reached back out to us, and we never reached out to her. Three 6 Mafia was now down to four members: DJ Paul, Lord Infamous, Crunchy Black, and me.

I felt Three 6 Mafia got stronger after Gangsta Boo's departure. Everyone was on the same page. When we'd go into the studio to make music, it was all good. No one was saying that they needed to change their rap, that they didn't want to rap a certain way. Everything was on point.

We all had egos and I never looked at it like I needed Gangsta Boo to make money. In fact, I never counted on any rapper in Three 6 Mafia for anything. When somebody would leave the crew, I would write a harder rap. I wanted my raps to be so good that the listener wouldn't miss our former members. I was so determined to succeed. It's like I was writing to prove that it didn't matter who left. They were not going to stop me. I was never going to let anybody stand in the way of my being successful.

No matter what would happen in my life, I'd always tell myself, "I don't give a fuck what happens. I'm going to come out on top."

I'm talented on my own and I know how to make songs. Plus, I didn't care who produced our former artists. They couldn't give them what Paul and I were delivering musically. But this business is not just about making songs. You also have to know how to promote them and get your music to the people. That's the mastermind game plan of the whole business. That's why it helps that I'm a real grinder, a real hustler. I know how to create opportunities.

"Y'all lose members, but you still come up," La Chat would say to me. She was right. We kept coming out with hit after hit after hit, so it wasn't like when David Ruffin left The Temptations. People thought the group was finished so they brought in other members to try to replace what Ruffin brought to the group's music. Yes, The Temptations were successful when Dennis Edwards joined, but the group's sound and style changed once Ruffin departed. Three 6 Mafia, on the other hand, was able to thrive and retain its ethos no matter who was leaving. DJ Paul and I were just stepping our game up as rappers.

Since the beginning of Three 6 Mafia, I had been telling everyone, "If you don't do it, somebody else will." Our crew was starting to see how real of a statement that was. They were living it. They'd hate when I'd get them up early in the morning to go to the radio station. "You're just kissing those White folks' asses," I heard they'd said about me. "It's *our label, our music, our money*," I'd think to myself. "It's Hypnotize Minds, and Columbia is backing it. *And they're putting up the big money.*"

For whatever reason, that didn't make sense to them, so I tried to put it a different way.

"Listen," I told the group, "we've got a hit record. If we go to the radio station, meet the program director, and promote our music, they might put our song in heavy rotation. If the radio spins go up, the record sales go up, and we make more money. Whether you want to do it or not, get your ass up and let's go."

The other group members hated me for that, but I always remembered where I came from, that I didn't have shit coming up. That's why I did it and why DJ Paul did it. That's how you had to work in order to be successful.

Unlike the others, La Chat saw that. It was also her time to shine.

Alan Grunblatt wasn't part of the Relativity Records transition to Loud Records. He had moved to Koch Records and was releasing albums with RZA, KRS-One, Fredro Starr, Ying Yang Twins, and others. We'd always done great business with Alan, so we got La Chat a deal with Koch and dropped her *Murder She Spoke* album October 23, 2001. It was another independent success.

As much as I wanted to focus on music, I couldn't. I had a family issue that I had to deal with. My dad was battling a gambling addiction. Pat and I were on the phone and he told me that our dad had taken out more than $70,000 from Pat's account. I couldn't believe it. Then I thought about my account. I looked and saw that my dad had taken about the same amount from my account. We had kept our father on our accounts in case we needed him to help us handle business. But when I looked, my father had taken $2,500 here, $10,000 there.

I didn't even want to add it up because the more I added, the more upset I was getting. I stopped looking at my statements because I was furious. Why was he doing this? Was he on drugs? I knew he had a gambling addiction, but damn.

The damage was done, though. While Pat was locked up, he was getting money from albums sales and publishing. But the money slowed up over time and my dad had taken more and more of Pat's money. When Pat got out of jail, I had to loan him some money to help him get back on his feet.

Fortunately, I had the money. It was overflowing. So was our creativity. While DJ Paul and I came up with ideas all the time, we also looked for inspiration from people in the game we admired. Back in June 1997, Master P shocked the rap game—and the entertainment business in general—by cowriting, codirecting, starring in, and financing his own movie, *I'm bout it*. He put it out direct to VHS on his own company, No Limit Films, which was distributed by Priority Records. Priority was the label that released Eazy-E, N.W.A, and Ice Cube, so they obviously had a lot of clout in the music industry.

Even though it was a revolutionary idea—to have a hit rapper make his own movie independently and release it straight to retail largely through record stores—Master P and Priority's plan worked out. Yeah, *I'm bout it* was a hood film and it starred mostly No Limit artists, but the movie was a hit, selling more than 250,000 units and proving to Hollywood that Master P had an audience, one that would support his movie. Later in 1997, he did a deal with Dimension Films and released *I Got the Hook-Up* starring Master P and A.J. Johnson. It grossed more than $10 million against a $3.5 million budget. Master P was a Hollywood power player, just like that.

People had been telling us for years that our music sounded like it should be in the movies. Since Master P represented his native New Orleans in *I'm bout it*, we wanted to do the same thing for Memphis. We wanted to make a movie and we had the money, so we did it. We got with Tyrone Mc-Clain and came up with the script, got with director Gil Green, went to Los Angeles, and filmed our own movie, *Choices*. We did all the music for the movie, too.

As our name grew, some of the biggest rappers in the industry wanted to work with us. DJ Paul and I had been producing ourselves and our artists for years, so I felt like I

This is my mother,
Shirley Jean Houston.
It's from when she was
17 and was taken in
1964 or so. My mom was
a faithful member of
the Pentecostal Temple
Church of God in Christ.
She sang in the choir
and served on the usher
board, too.

This is my father,
Jordan Houston Jr.
It's from 1968. My dad
was a traveling minister,
but he also served in
the US Army.

Top: Here I am as a kid posing with a toy gun.

Bottom: I had a great time growing up with my brother, Patrick, and my sisters Carol (left) and Cheryl. Here, I'm all smiles in the late 1970s.

Opposite Top Left: I liked posing for pictures as a kid. Here, I'm with my sister Carol and my brother, Patrick. We took this one back in May 1977.

Opposite Top Right: Check out my smile in this photo. I've always felt comfortable in front of the camera.

Opposite Bottom: The shadows add a lot of character to this photo of my brother, Patrick; my sister Carol; and me.

AUTHOR COLLECTION

AUTHOR COLLECTION

Top: When I was growing up, my father, Jordan Houston Jr., spent a lot of time on the road. He was a traveling minister. When he was home, everyone was so happy. You can see the happiness in the eyes of my father, my sisters Cheryl and Carol, and me.

Bottom: My mom worked as a librarian when I was growing up. She got me books on a variety of topics, from the music industry to history. I loved reading. In this picture from 1990 or so, I'm in front of books in the library at Northside High School, which is where I went to school.

Opposite Top: Even though I said my ambition was to be a lawyer, I never really wanted to be one. It just sounded like the right thing to say. As you can see, I'm wearing my headphones and acting as if I'm scratching. I was focused on music and being a DJ.

Opposite Bottom: I didn't need a cane in order to walk. Sometimes, though, I would use one because I thought using it made me look cool. This photo is from my 1992 calendar.

Presenting _Jordan (Juicy "J") Houston_

Age _18_ Grade _12_ Ambition _Lawyer_

Student of Northside Photo Class

JANUARY	JULY
S M T W T F S	S M T W T F S
1 2 3 4	1 2 3 4
5 6 7 8 9 10 11	5 6 7 8 9 10 11
12 13 14 15 16 17 18	12 13 14 15 16 17 18
19 20 21 22 23 24 25	19 20 21 22 23 24 25
26 27 28 29 30 31	26 27 28 29 30 31 25

FEBRUARY	AUGUST
S M T W T F S	S M T W T F S
1	1
2 3 4 5 6 7 8	2 3 4 5 6 7 8
9 10 11 12 13 14 15	9 10 11 12 13 14 15
16 17 18 19 20 21 22	16 17 18 19 20 21 22
23 24 25 26 27 28 29	23 24 25 26 27 28 29
	30 31

1

MARCH	SEPTEMBER
S M T W T F S	S M T W T F S
1 2 3 4 5 6 7	1 2 3 4 5
8 9 10 11 12 13 14	6 7 8 9 10 11 12
15 16 17 18 19 20 21	13 14 15 16 17 18 19
22 23 24 25 26 27 28	20 21 22 23 24 25 26
29 30 31	27 28 29 30

9

APRIL	OCTOBER
S M T W T F S	S M T W T F S
1 2 3 4	1 2 3
5 6 7 8 9 10 11	4 5 6 7 8 9 10
12 13 14 15 16 17 18	11 12 13 14 15 16 17
19 20 21 22 23 24 25	18 19 20 21 22 23 24
18 29 30	25 26 27 28 29 30 31

9

MAY	NOVEMBER
T W T F S	S M T W T F S
1 2	1 2 3 4 5 6 7
5 6 7 8 9	8 9 10 11 12 13 14
12 13 14 15 16	15 16 17 18 19 20 21
19 20 21 22 23	22 23 24 25 26 27 28
26 27 28 29 30	29 30 1

2

JUNE	DECEMBER
T W T F S	S M T W T F S
2 3 4 5 6	1 2 3 4 5 18
9 10 11 12 13	6 7 8 9 10 11 12 5
16 17 18 19 20	13 14 15 16 17 18 19
23 24 25 26 27	20 21 22 23 24 25 26
30	27 28 29 30 31

Top: I grew up idolizing DJ Jazzy Jeff and trying to mimic his moves, including being able to scratch behind my back. That's what I'm doing here in this photo from 1991 or so.

Bottom: This is the flyer for my *Chronicles of The Juice Manne* mixtape that I self-released in 1994. Lil Noid is in the background of the photo, too. He was a member of Backyard Posse, the group that spawned Three 6 Mafia.

Top: This is my hand-drawn flyer for "Juicy J's Place" back in 1994. I wanted my parties to be inclusive, so I wrote "Orange Mound," "Black Haven," "North Memphis" and other spots on my flyers to make people from different neighborhoods want to come through.

Bottom: Check out one of my early Juicy "J" business cards. I was proud to put the Hypnotize Minds logo next to the one for our partner, Relativity Records. We put out a lot of great albums with Relativity from 1997–1999.

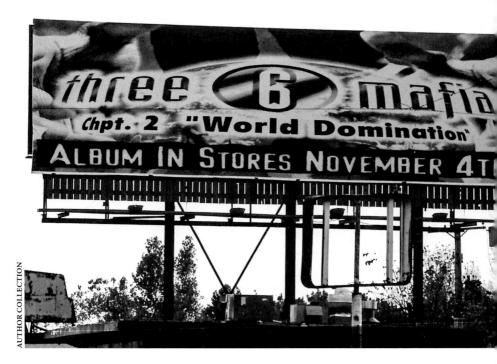

Top: We went all out to promote ourselves back in the day. This is a photo of a billboard promoting Three 6 Mafia in 1997. Our *Chpt. 2: "World Domination"* album was our first to earn gold status. It sold more than 500,000 units.

Bottom: I was on a roll in 1999 thanks to Three 6 Mafia's deal with Relativity Records, a major label based in New York. Here, I'm sharing a happy moment with my mom in Memphis.

Opposite Top: Check out my handwritten lyrics from the Tear Da Club Up Thugs song "Hypnotize Cash Money." It was on the *CrazyNDaLazDayz* album.

Opposite Bottom: The bigger we got, the more we got to travel. In 1999, Project Pat, DJ Paul and I were hanging out at the Sofitel Hotel in Beverly Hills, California. We hit the West Coast to promote Project Pat's *Ghetty Green* LP.

Its the Juice coming up out da dark, from my part
North Memphis Niggaz always hard and we start shss
wit these coward play haters, we anit no traters
But some hustlers and some chese Chasers
Pass that Green if you a friend ta me
About that paper

You see BigeyTricce kill a fifth of Hennsee
get Buk wild in da club thats how we be
All gang Niggiz throw them thangs and show
them teeth (Playa WAY YA Aden (Hypnotize Cash Money)

Top: Here I am in Miami in 2000 with Project Pat, DJ Paul, Lord Infamous, and Gangsta Boo. You can see in this photo that we had no idea we were on the verge of breaking through to the mainstream with the song and video for "Sippin' On Some Syrup."

Bottom: Man, this could have been an album cover. DJ Paul and I are in front of our rides and next to our custom Hypnotize Minds car. We took this in 2005 or so in front of our Hypnotize Minds Studios.

AUTHOR COLLECTION

AUTHOR COLLECTION

Top: We had this Chevy custom-painted with the Hypnotize Minds logo. On this day, it was in front of our Hypnotize Minds Studios.

Bottom: DJ Paul and I were hanging out with Soren Baker at Three 6 Mafia's Hollywood Hills home back in 2006. Soren was one of the first—if not *the* first—national writers to report on Three 6 Mafia, so he was the perfect person to coauthor *Chronicles of The Juice Man* with me. Check out Soren holding the Oscars DJ Paul and I won for Best Original Song for "It's Hard Out Here for A Pimp" from *Hustle & Flow.*

I loved
Kobe Bryant's
game and got
to meet him
back in 2007.
That was a
special moment.

I've been able to
travel the world.
Check me out
in front of
Mt. Rushmore
back in 2007.

The Rock is an icon. I got to meet him in 2015.

I love doing shows. Back in 2014 or so, I was on the road chopping it up with Berner, Loody Boy, MGK, Wiz Khalifa and Chevy Woods.

I collaborated with 21 Savage on DJ Scream's "Lit." We took this photo in 2019 or so.

Logic and I have become great friends. This picture is from the "1995" video shoot in Utah in 2020. Logic and I recorded a collaborative album together. Logic produced all the songs.

Project Pat and I grew up in Memphis and are now known around the world. We've come a long way. Here we are in Conway Studios in Los Angeles in 2021.

I worked on my collaborative album with Logic at Encore Studios in Burbank, California. I took this picture on January 23, 2023, while we were recording the project.

Top: My love for my children is infinite. Kamai and Myle bring me endless joy.

Bottom: My wife Regina and I have celebrated a lot of great times over the years. Here we are at Drai's Nightclub in Las Vegas in early 2023.

knew the Memphis flow. I was about to learn that I needed to adjust my thinking for other artists.

Ludacris was such a lyricist that I didn't know how he was going to start his rap off when he did "Dis Bitch, Dat Hoe," a song he did for the *Choices* soundtrack with Three 6 Mafia and Project Pat. Ludacris was a real character on that song, elongating his words in a distinctive way. He was like, "Ludacriiiiiiiiiiiis." I thought it was amazing.

The rest of the *Choices* soundtrack was filled with songs from Hypnotize Minds artists. DJ Paul, La Chat, and I did "2-Way Freak," a nod to the two-way pagers that were popular at the time. We also did the macabre "Mean Mug" with La Chat, while our artist T-Rock had the great solo song "Slang & Serve."

The *Choices* movie and its soundtrack were hits as soon as they dropped in November 2001.

That same month, Three 6 Mafia appeared on "Go 2 Sleep," a song from Ludacris' *Word Of Mouf* album. It sold more than 3 million copies in less than a year, making it the biggest project we'd been a part of to that point.

That type of exposure gave us even more reason to release nationally the underground independent music people around the country hadn't heard to that point. Both DJ Paul and I were sitting on so much of our own music. We decided to drop solo independent projects back-to-back.

Whenever Paul and I would put out our own projects through Select-O-Hits, we wouldn't use Hypnotize Minds as the company. We kept things separate, which is why he released his *Underground Vol. 16 For Da Summa* album via his D. Evil Musik and KOM Music companies on May 21, 2002. For my *Chronicles of the Juice Man* album, I released it via North North Records on July 16, 2002. I was paying homage to North Memphis with the company's name.

Since I grew up in the church, I felt that everything that I did and anything good that happened to me was God's gift. Even sometimes the bad stuff I experienced, I felt like He was giving me a sign to slow down. Good or bad, when things happened in my life, I thought it was because of Him. That's why on the back cover of *Chronicles of the Juice Man*, I included a Bible verse, Revelation Chapter 1, Verse 3. *"Blessed is the one who reads aloud the words of this prophecy, and blessed are those who hear it and take to heart what is written in it, because the time is near."*

I know that may seem crazy coming from a guy in a group called Three 6 Mafia, but I did it because I felt like we needed that on there. After everything we'd talked about on our albums, and all the pain, suffering, and drugs, I wanted to put some good words on there, to offer somebody some inspiration if they happened to read it.

Inspiration really does come from everywhere. As much as I know music, I can never be sure what is going to catch an artist's ear. When we were playing beats for Ludacris, I skipped over the beat that he ended up using for "Diamond In The Back." I didn't think he'd like it because I was used to hearing him make turn-up music, but he had heard the intro and asked me to go back to it. Luda ended up putting "Diamond In The Back" on his 2003 album, *Chicken-N-Beer*, and making it a single with a video, too. The project moved more than 2 million units, going double platinum.

I felt like we had some of the hardest beats out there, so getting calls from titans in the game gave me a sense of validation. Working with other artists was a huge accomplishment for DJ Paul and me. I'd always wanted to work with other superstar artists. It made me feel like we were reaching Quincy Jones status. Plus, it was another check. It was different income but still from music.

Sometimes the artists don't pick the beats you think are perfect for them. I told Ludacris that the beat that ended up being "Wolf Wolf" was for him. He dragged his feet and we ended up putting "Wolf Wolf" on our *Da Unbreakables* album.

DJ Paul and I weren't just sending out beats. In order to work with an artist, we'd either have to like them or have a relationship with them. Then we'd have them come to our studio, or we'd meet them somewhere. Occasionally, we'd put some beats on a CD and FedEx them to the artist. That's how we started getting our beats placed on songs for Young Buck, T.I., OutKast, Mike Jones, Lil' Flip, Paul Wall, and others.

When people would talk to us, they couldn't understand how we were able to work with these artists or get them on our songs and in our videos. What people on the outside looking in didn't get was that these were our friends and we knew them. It was deeper than rap.

By 2003, we had sold millions of records and made millions of dollars. Our independent success continued with releases from Da Headbussaz, our collaborative group with Fiend, and albums from our protégés Lil Wyte and Frayser Boy, both of whom were from Memphis. Lil Wyte's debut album, *Doubt Me Now*, in particular was a major success, selling more than 100,000 units independently. The Hypnotize Minds money train was rolling.

When you start making money, unfortunately, you start getting more money for drugs. When the drug use started going up, things started getting real crazy and getting out of control with the group.

We would travel together and I used to ride in the car with Lord Infamous and Crunchy Black. One day in 2003, we were on the road promoting our *Da Unbreakables* album. Things were not going well with the group. DJ Paul told me he might leave Three 6 Mafia if the project wasn't successful. It seemed like everyone in the group—Paul, Lord, Crunchy, and I—was giving up hope. It didn't help that *Da Unbreakables* didn't come out the gate strong like *When The Smoke Clears: Sixty 6, Sixty 1* dropped.

At that time, Columbia Records didn't push us. They had absorbed Loud Records and weren't used to promoting hard-core street rap like Three 6 Mafia. Columbia would just throw the albums out and see what happened. *Da Unbreakables* lead single, "Ridin Spinners," features Lil' Flip. I was disappointed the label wasn't pushing us, but one day a label rep called me and said we were getting lots of radio play in markets where Lil' Flip was popular. It was great to hear that, but it seemed like the song was taking off organically rather than getting true support from Columbia.

The group was having a hard time, and we got pulled over by the police during a promo run. Lord Infamous— who had OD'd at the "Ridin Spinners" video shoot—had so much fuckin' cocaine in his pocket, as well as pills and heroin. The cops didn't find anything. After that, I looked at Lord's jacket. I said, "Dude, look at your pocket."

He was like, "Oh, man. I'm so glad that officer didn't find that, man." He didn't even realize he had so many drugs stashed in his pocket.

So I said to myself, "If I get pulled over with these dudes and they got all these unregistered guns and all this cocaine, that's a federal charge. I'll go to jail because I'm in the car with these clowns." I was okay with taking my chances with the guns because we needed them, but not the drugs. Everyone that I knew that had done coke, they went downhill. They fell and they fell fast. That wasn't going to happen to me.

For years I'd been acting like a daddy to the rest of Three 6 Mafia. I knew things had to change. After getting pulled over like that, I bought my own van. I got the feeling that certain members of the group felt like I thought I was too good for them and didn't like being around them. They were right. I didn't like being around them when they were using drugs. I didn't begrudge the use of drugs. Everyone makes their own choices. Some people do drugs. Some people go to church. People do what they want to do. I chose not to do the drugs they were doing and to ride by myself. I didn't want to get pulled over and get incarcerated because of them. I can't make money in jail. I always felt that nobody was going to stop me from fulfilling my dream. No, sir.

I had to tell Paul that I wasn't riding with Crunchy, that I wasn't riding with Lord. Paul kept riding with them, but eventually even he couldn't take it and started pulling away from the crew. He told them to get their own car, that they had to get themselves to our shows.

Lord was a serious drug addict. He would snort some powder, sip some syrup, take some pills. He'd often do them all at once—like he mentioned in his songs, he was a speedball king—and end up passed out at a club with wads of money hanging out of his pockets.

Lord would also get into all kinds of disagreements. He got into a fight with one of our guitar players over drugs.

Word on the street was that Lord would be seen in random spots and was getting robbed all the time. One time, Pat found out who'd robbed Lord in South Memphis. Pat was going to go shoot them, but we were able to calm him down.

When he wasn't getting robbed, Lord Infamous was having other serious problems. He'd fall asleep in his car, run red lights. Thanks to our success, he had bought a truck with these big exhaust pipes. He got pulled over and got into a fight with a female police officer. As they were fighting, she put his hand on the pipes, severely burning him.

That type of thing was normal for Lord. He was so gone. Heroin got a hold of him, just like it had Ray Charles. There was no return. Lord was never able to kick that drug habit.

I remember hearing Mike Tyson talk about his life. All the stuff that he did—the fights outside the ring, his arrests, the drama, going to jail—that's just who he was at the time. Mike accepted that. I try not to judge people, but with the members of Three 6 Mafia, I had to learn how to deal with them and their wild mood swings.

When Lord was on the drugs, I could never tell when he was going to lash out at me. One time he was in the studio with me. Paul caught him in the bathroom doing heroin and threw it out. Then Lord snapped. "Juicy J. Fuck YOU! AHHHH! Fuck Project Pat!"

We kicked Lord Infamous out of the studio. I didn't take what he was saying personally. I knew he was a drug head and not in his right mind. Sometimes I'd have to wake him up in his hotel room because he was knocked out from the drugs. So many times I'd taken his drugs and thrown them away. I told him I didn't want him to die off drugs and begged him to stop.

Another time, I picked Lord up from his house and drove him around South Memphis. I was begging him to go to rehab, but he couldn't leave it alone. He went off on me in the studio soon after that and I had security kick him out. Lord came back a week later and apologized for being high, but it looked to me like he was *high* as he was telling me this. I told him that I knew he was high and to just go lay his verse. At least he would apologize. I just wanted to finish making the song. It was sad, but I had to focus.

I remember the last time I gave him a check. About two hours later, we got a call that he was in the hospital. He had passed out behind the wheel. Half of the money I gave him was gone. There was nothing else I could do at that point. A person really has to want to get off the drugs themselves.

For years, drugs had been pulling Lord Infamous away, causing him to gradually fade from the group. Since the beginning, I looked at him as a leader of Three 6 Mafia in a way. He was our lead voice, a true lyricist with so much style and so many flows, just like Ice Cube had been for N.W.A.

But Lord Infamous just stopped showing up at the studio. I'd ask Paul if he knew where Lord was. Paul would say he didn't know. Even though I felt like he was the voice of Three 6 Mafia, when he started slacking, other voices had to step up. Like I'd done before, I wrote the hardest verses I could think of.

Now it was 2004 and Lord Infamous had left the group. It broke my heart because if it were up to me, we could have worked through everybody's issues, and Koopsta Knicca, Gangsta Boo, and Lord Infamous would have still been in

Three 6 Mafia. That's not what happened, though. With each one of them, it had gotten to the point where I had to put my hands up and give up. Three 6 Mafia was down to three members: DJ Paul, Crunchy Black, and me.

I hated seeing Lord Infamous deteriorate, but I felt in my heart nobody was going to stop me or the group. We had too much momentum. When we did the *Most Known Unknown* album in 2005, we decided to make a Tennessee anthem, so we connected with my longtime friends 8Ball & MJG and Nashville rapper and G-Unit member Young Buck for "Stay Fly."

The song was another example of Three 6 Mafia's diversity. We used a sped-up sample of Willie Hutch's "Tell Me Why Has Our Love Turned Cold" as the musical foundation of the song. Even though "Stay Fly" was fast, it wasn't crunk or the dark, devil wave like some of our early music. It had a totally different and soulful vibe. Featuring 8Ball & MJG and Young Buck on it was a brilliant move, too. People weren't expecting that. Three 6 Mafia continued to evolve, which had been a hallmark of our career and one of the reasons for our success.

"Stay Fly" became an anthem and one of our biggest songs, with sales of more than 2 million mastertones. That's when people would buy songs and use them for their ringtones for their incoming calls.

"Stay Fly" took off so quickly that we had to rush to put *Most Known Unknown* together. In order to save time, DJ Paul and I decided to take some of the songs we'd been recording for a Crunchy Black solo album and put them on *Most Known Unknown*. Three 6 Mafia had always been our priority, but Crunchy Black wasn't happy. Plus, more than ever, people started telling Crunchy that he was the hardest member of the group and that they loved how he flowed.

It was a bad combination, but things were moving so fast that DJ Paul and I didn't worry too much about Crunchy's concerns at the time. We had to hit the road to maximize our opportunities to make "Stay Fly" a smash.

"Stay Fly" made us return to the skies. The song was so popular and we were in such demand that Three 6 Mafia started flying again. I was so scared, but I knew we had to do it in order to keep hustling.

My return to flying wasn't totally smooth. I'd often think about how people flew planes into buildings. On the one hand, I wanted to be alert. I also needed to relax. For protection and good luck, I flew with a Bible in my bag at all times. That didn't take away my nervousness, though, so I started taking Xanax to try to calm my nerves and my paranoia when we were flying. Even though I wasn't supposed to, I'd also drink alcohol when I would pop a pill. Both are depressants and I was in real risk of my heart stopping, but they made me feel good.

Once I got enamored with taking Xanax on our flights, I started taking them other times, too. I usually took them on the low. I wanted to find a way to enjoy our success and, as foolish as it was, this was a way I could do it.

Our other main single from the LP, "Poppin' My Collar," sounds much different than what I had originally set out to do. I envisioned the song as just a drumbeat and bass, and no other music. No one else liked the idea, though. I was upset, so I put the song to the side.

As we were making *Most Known Unknown*, I decided to put "Poppin' My Collar" back on there. Now, though, I decided I'd build the music off a sample of Willie Hutch's

"Theme Of The Mack" since everyone around me was so adamant about it. I used the technique I started way back on my underground mixtapes. I'd take a soul sample and put a hood hook over it. At this time, we'd been working with Mobile, Alabama, rapper Mr. Bigg (aka The Last Mr. Bigg). When I listened to his a cappellas, I realized he'd often say some hard shit. At first, I was thinking about sampling his voice for a song on the debut album from our latest protégé and Hypnotize Minds artist Chrome. But then I thought the idea I had for the Mr. Bigg a cappella would work for the "Poppin' My Collar" chorus.

I took two different lines and built the chorus from Mr. Bigg's rhymes: *"Ever since I can remember, I've been poppin' my collar/Poppin' poppin' my collar/Poppin' poppin' my collar/ Ever since I can remember I've been working these hoes and they betta put my money in my hand."*

While I thought it was a good song, I didn't think "Poppin' My Collar" was a hit. We visited a radio station in Miami and the program director told me it was the one. Columbia Records told me the same thing, but I didn't believe them.

I was really nervous about making "Poppin' My Collar" a Three 6 Mafia single. But everybody else was right and I was wrong. It was another smash hit for the group. It peaked at No. 21 on the Billboard Hot 100 and sold more than 1 million mastertones, too. Those sales helped push *Most Known Unknown* to platinum status, too. More than a decade after we put out *Mystic Stylez* on Select-O-Hits, Three 6 Mafia had its second million-selling album.

Regardless of who was in the group, what type of song we made, or who we collaborated with, Three 6 Mafia was a legitimate force, a true brand, a musical powerhouse.

Around this time, something we did a few years earlier was about to pay off for us. Back in 2000, we were in LA shooting our movie, *Choices*. John Singleton heard about it and stopped by the set. He was blown away that we were some Memphis dudes in California shooting a real movie on 16-millimeter film and everything. He asked us to write a song for his upcoming movie *Baby Boy*. This is the same guy who wrote and directed *Boyz n the Hood*, so of course we were going to do it.

We did "Baby Mama" with our artist La Chat. That song really meant something to me even though I didn't have any kids, because a lot of people I was around had children, and there always seemed to be some baby mama drama. I had heard so many horror stories about baby mamas *and* baby daddies. The song almost wrote itself.

John loved "Baby Mama" and put it throughout the movie. He also told us he wanted to put La Chat in one of his movies. He'd tell us, "She needs to be seen, man, because she's so hood."

In 2004, when John started working on *Hustle & Flow* in Memphis, he called us up and told us he wanted us to do all the music for the movie. He and writer-director Craig Brewer came to the studio and told us about the script, that it focused on a pimp who was having a hard time trying to be a rapper. He's got a couple of chicks and he's going through a lot of drama. Right there, we came up with the idea for "It's Hard Out Here For A Pimp." We didn't have a beat or anything. We just said, "It's hard out here for a pimp." The song came together pretty naturally.

What I loved about the process of making "It's Hard Out Here For A Pimp," though, was the challenge. The adrenaline, I love it. I wanted to nail the song. Sure, I'd shot a couple of independent movies (*Choices II: The Setup* and *Clean Up Men*) at that point with Three 6 Mafia, but this was different. I wanted to prove to myself, and others, that I could do anything musically.

When John and Craig gave us the script, I was expecting something different. I'm from Memphis, so I was thinking there was going to be a lot of shooting, niggas getting their heads blown off, and lots of pimping, but there wasn't much of that in there. However, I thought it would be big because it was on some real-life story. Djay, the pimp portrayed by Terrence Howard, he goes to jail at the end of the day. Even though he got his song played on the radio, it wasn't a happy ending. He didn't become a star and sell 20 million records. He just got his song played on Memphis radio and he was in jail. Some movies are pretty unbelievable, but you could watch *Hustle & Flow* and see that happening.

John told me he put up about $2 million of his own money to make *Hustle & Flow*. It was low-budget, and John had to cut corners to make it, but he sold it to Paramount Pictures and MTV Films at Sundance for $9 million. That was the biggest sale in the festival's history and the movie went on to gross more than $23 million at the box office. That was just the beginning of the good news.

One day, I got a call at 5 a.m. John Singleton and Craig Brewer were on the line. They were screaming, "You just got nominated for a muthafuckin' Oscar, man."

"It's Hard Out Here For A Pimp" was nominated for Best Original Song at the 2006 Oscars. It was surreal. It didn't make sense to me. I had grown up watching the Oscars and seeing Denzel Washington, Halle Berry, and all these Black actors win. When we got nominated for the Oscar, my phone was ringing so much. Even though I didn't think we had a chance to win, I felt like we were unstoppable.

I was also thinking about our next move, how we were going to level up.

DJ Paul, Frayser Boy, and I showed up at the Kodak Theatre in Los Angeles on March 5, 2006, with no expectations. After we performed, we felt like we'd already won. Three 6 Mafia had performed at the Oscars. That was beyond our comprehension.

After our performance, we were backstage about to head to the bar. Then a bunch of people started saying, "Where are you going? You better stand here in case they say your name." We didn't like it when people were saying that because we thought they were playing with us.

But then Queen Latifah announced that "It's Hard Out Here For A Pimp" had won Original Song at the 2006 Oscars. We couldn't believe it. Our lives flipped in that instant, opening a new world to us.

Winning the Oscar ended up being one of the best and most painful experiences of my life. On one hand, I felt like getting that statue proved that we were the shit. We had been a secret weapon for so long. Now we had the biggest validation of them all.

On the other hand, we had just been handed our statues and Gayle King was interviewing us. "I guess it's a sad day," she said to us. I was smiling, happy to be there and basking in the moment, so I didn't know what she was talking about. She was saying that Three 6 Mafia winning an Oscar was a sad day. It was so awkward, but then she just started interviewing us as if she hadn't *just* said that. I was focused on answering her questions, so I didn't ask her what she meant.

On the way out of the Kodak Theatre, we saw Will Smith. He wasn't happy for us. "I'm just upset that y'all got one before me," he told me. As someone who grew up loving his music, television shows, and movies, that hurt more than anyone could imagine.

When we got to the after-parties, John Travolta congratulated us, and Jamie Foxx showed us a lot of love. I turned around and Steven Spielberg was standing right next to me, lighting up a cigar. "Congratulations," he told us.

Three 6 Mafia went by Prince's house, but he wouldn't let us in. Then we hit the *Vanity Fair* party and the vibe was off. "You're a lucky-ass bitch," Taye Diggs said to me. It wasn't just him, either. So many Black people were looking at us sideways, like "Fuck y'all niggas." John Singleton pulled me to the side. "You feel that *hate*?" he asked me. It was so crazy that John *felt* it, too. "They're just mad," he said, "'cause they don't have one."

This isn't totally true, of course, but it seemed like all the Black folk were hating on us and all the White people were happy for us. It was the weirdest shit I'd ever seen in my life. I was totally shocked. You would think that your own people would support you. No. They didn't. The shit was Hollywood as fuck.

Columbia Records, on the other hand, took care of us. They put us in a much better hotel. Housekeeping told us that there was a red button on the wall. All we had to do was hit it and let them know whatever we wanted and they'd get it for us. I stayed in that hotel room for two or three weeks, really living it up, partying, drinking, flying girls in and out of town.

Even though I was living it up in LA, one thing I didn't do was watch our Oscar performance over and over again. After I perform, I move on. I don't want to watch myself because I know how I am. It will turn into an "I should have done this. I should have done that" type of session. I never want to get bogged down with those types of thoughts. So, I probably only watched our Oscar performance twice. I was too busy, anyway.

After we won that Oscar, everybody wanted to hang out with the Oscar winners. Sure, we could have gone back to Memphis and worked, but you only live once and we wanted to live this experience to the fullest. We'd be at Paris Hilton's house, the Playboy Mansion. It was nothing to see naked girls walking around. Paris Hilton invited Paul and me to a club. I met Serena Williams and Kim Kardashian there. Two months later, I started dating Serena. Paul and I were drunk and high all the time, spending our time at every strip club, every bar.

Overnight, Three 6 Mafia had gone from doing underground shows to partying with Quentin Tarantino and George Clooney and sitting next to Tim Burton at events. Dolly Parton wrote a letter congratulating us on winning an Oscar. DJ Paul framed that.

We had a meeting with Stan Lee. He was telling us that when he was making Marvel Comics, he never thought it would amount to anything. Eventually, he got to the point where he was making good money, but his business really exploded when they gave his characters movies and television shows, from Spider-Man and X-Men to The Incredible Hulk and Iron Man.

It sounded similar to what Three 6 Mafia was experiencing with our Oscar win. It was like a light switch had been flipped and our lives had changed. Stan Lee was interested in doing a cartoon with us, but unfortunately nothing materialized.

Sylvester Stallone invited us to his house. "Congratulations," he said once we arrived. "It goes fast." That stuck in my head. I realized that we should hustle and try to win another Oscar.

Stallone was right. I was in the middle of the best time of my life, but all wasn't right. Three 6 Mafia was more famous than we could have ever imagined, but we lost focus. Hollywood was beautiful and we had more money than we knew what to do with.

Every time we went to Memphis, we hurried back to Los Angeles as fast as we possibly could. We loved Memphis, but we were over it. My vision of myself in Memphis wasn't a good one. I was too worried about getting caught up in some street shit and needing to shoot someone. I saw more hate. LA was much more our speed at the time. We were too enamored with the new parties, drugs, and A-list celebrity lifestyle.

In the midst of all that, my "Fuck it" and "Fear" sides were still active. I had been partying so much that every now and then I'd be at a party and think I was about to go over the edge. When this would happen, I would take my cup and pour my liquor out, flush my lean down the toilet, throw my Xanax out the window. I never wanted to get to a point where I couldn't function. My "Fear" side was forcing me to stay focused. It was a real battle. But I saw how other people acted when they were on drugs. I never wanted to be like that.

I'd be at parties like that one in Holmby Hills and people would be walking around with flavored cocaine. I saw it, but I didn't try it. Every time I'd see something like that, I'd think of Len Bias.

There were other issues, too. Even though I thought we had talked it out, my father took more money from me.

My father and I got into my white Range Rover and talked again. We had the statements coming to my mother's house and when my father looked at them, he told me he'd never seen that much money before. He said he just couldn't help himself. As we talked, my father cried. He seemed almost as upset as I was.

As I calmed down and thought about the situation, I had to laugh to myself. Even though I had never told my dad about this, I remember how I used to steal money out of his wallet. It wasn't big money, maybe $5 here or $10 there. I guess this was his way—or maybe just karma's way—of getting me back.

I was more disappointed than mad, so the next time I saw my dad, I gave him some more money. He asked why I would do that since he owed me money. I told him that I felt like he needed the money. If he needed anything, I told him he could call me and I would give it to him. I've always been there for my family, just as they've always been there for me. I've got a big heart. I just didn't want my dad taking money out of my account or Pat's account.

Still, it was depressing. But I just tried to let it go. We had gone from Three 6 Mafia to pop stars. We'd won an Oscar. I felt like I could do anything. I couldn't have been more wrong.

CHAPTER
8

DON'T CHA GET MAD

RIGHT BEFORE WE MOVED to LA, we were just making music and there wasn't a lot of cocaine around— not like there used to be back in the early and mid-1990s. So, I felt like everybody was kind of on the same page. But after the Oscar, man, a lot of shit changed. People just started coming at us. I heard, "If you ever need anything, I've got a doctor for you," so many times. Everybody's selling something in LA.

I had so many plugs, and I was using them. I had so much syrup and a whole cabinet full of pills. It was taking a toll on me. In order to go onstage, I had to have these drugs in my body. On the one hand, I was having the time of my life. We were selling out shows and making a lot of money. On the other hand, I was empty.

I was a different person now. Paul was, too. I had something to do with that and Paul had something to do with that. We were older and we were making a lot of money. Crunchy Black was still stuck in the past. He was refusing to use a BlackBerry even though the Oscars gave us each a free one. I had explained how easy it was to use and how helpful it was going to be. I told him once he set up an e-mail account I could just send him the actual tour itinerary. Plus, he could see everything for himself instead of me having to call him all the time.

Crunchy was also used to me calling him, getting him up in the morning. When I told him he'd have to get a BlackBerry and that someone from either Loud or its parent company Columbia Records would e-mail him our itinerary, he didn't want to do that. He wanted me to just call him. I told him no. Crunchy Black was so against using a BlackBerry that he said he was going to have his friend Booger do it for him.

Unfortunately, that wasn't the only issue. When Three 6 Mafia went to New York for business, I decided to stay at The Carlyle because I'd gotten a gift card in my Oscar gift bag. Crunchy was staying at a different hotel and they wanted him to put down a credit card for incidentals. They explained to him that he'd have to put $300 down—$100 for each day of his stay—and once he checked out of the room and everything was good, he'd get his $300 back. He didn't want that, so someone from Columbia Records called me and explained the situation to me. I was furious. The label rep got us on three-way and I told Crunchy that he must be out of his fuckin' mind. Crunchy said he wanted me to cover the incidentals for his hotel room and put my card down, but I knew he had $10,000 cash in his pocket.

I was livid. I told Crunchy that things had changed, that we were getting bigger and we had to do things the right way. We had shows, tours, a lot of big things coming up. I wasn't going to be able to come to do everything for him anymore. Crunchy wasn't trying to hear it, so I hung the phone up on him. I couldn't believe it.

Later that day, I saw Crunchy Black at his hotel. He came up to me with tears in his eyes and told me he was going to try to get off the dope, that he was going to get some help. But he was *high*. I looked him dead in his eyes and told him I couldn't believe anything he was saying. "Go sober up and then we can have a real conversation about how we can help you get off the drugs," I told him.

During the trip, I was in the studio. That morning, I'd been calling and texting Crunchy. His phone was off, and I asked around but no one had seen him. I called over to his hotel and the doorman said he'd seen him, but that Crunchy had left and was going back to Memphis. He'd changed his number. That was it. I couldn't believe it. Crunchy Black had left Three 6 Mafia. Three 6 Mafia was down to two members: DJ Paul and me.

We had just won an Oscar and had a TV show with MTV on the table. Crunchy was set to get a third of the money from our show. We also had tours lined up and he was going to get a third of that money, too, because he'd been a member of Three 6 Mafia. We treated our people right. He was given a great opportunity with more money and more shine. I thought that would have made him happy.

Crunchy Black, though, he felt like things were changing. He thought that Paul was abandoning him. They were road dogs. Crunchy took it personally when Paul distanced himself from Crunchy and wouldn't ride to the shows with him anymore. The drug use and our egos were truly taking their toll.

Crunchy had been feeling this way for a while and it was finally too much for him to stomach. I remember thinking it was strange that after we won the Oscar, he just left. He didn't go with us to any parties. The fame had been getting to him. I'd been seeing in his eyes that he was troubled.

As the reality kicked in, I was stunned. I was going to miss Crunchy Black's dancing and his flavor. But I remember thinking that we didn't need Crunchy Black, that he was the weakest link of Three 6 Mafia.

In interviews I've seen Crunchy Black say a lot of powerful things about his drug abuse, about how he shouldn't have left the group, about how he should have called DJ Paul and me, about how I was like the Godfather for the group. It was nice hearing him explain these things, especially how I wanted him to get off the drugs and how I tried to help him get off drugs.

Project Pat was in the studio with me the morning I found out Crunchy Black had left Three 6 Mafia. I told Pat that I wanted him to be in the group.

"Nah. I can't do that," Project Pat said to me.

I was in disbelief. "You're about to get a third of our TV money if you're in Three 6 Mafia," I replied. "Stop playing."

"Nah, man," Pat said. "I'm good." Pat's mental peace meant more to him than getting a big payday.

As I'd done every time someone left the group, I tried to step my rapping up. I was hanging out with Serena Williams' sister Lyndrea. We would make music, and when she'd come by my house, she was always complimenting me on my raps. I was trying out so many different flows and styles. I knew it was just going to be Paul and me on the songs, so I wanted to bring as much energy as possible to the mic.

Crunchy Black's issues had been one thing. DJ Paul and I were in different realities, too. I had a house in Memphis chilling on four acres of land that I had built from the ground up, but I drove down the street in LA, saw this $2 million house, and I just bought it. I was like, "I'm never going back to Memphis. Fuck that house."

I also felt safer in Los Angeles than Memphis. At home, I was always looking over my shoulder. Memphis is a dark city, literally and figuratively. It rains and you have thunderstorms. You never knew who was plotting to get you, to rob you. I didn't want to be in Memphis and get into some situation where I had to kill somebody. Every time we had another hit or some success, people would try to test us. We had a whole posse of gangsters on standby ready for whatever. Things had gotten to that point.

By comparison, life in LA was a breeze. In California, it's sunny and warm almost all the time. I could finally rest and get some sleep. DJ Paul and I were away from all the hate in Memphis and we were able to indulge in our newfound celebrity.

That was all just on the surface, though. In addition to being literally drunk on alcohol and high on drugs, I was drunk on the power I thought I had. Every time I got off stage, I was angry. I told my lawyer anything anyone wanted us to do would cost $250,000 and up. Charge the shit out of people for shows, features, beats, I told him. If the label called, tell them we want more money than whatever they were offering. I was terrible.

To make matters worse, our lawyer Aaron Rosenberg, as amazing as he was, was too aggressive—even for me.

People would tell me how our lawyer was fucking things up for us. But later when we thought about it, he was really looking out for our best interests. Coming from the South, we may arrive with our guns out, but we'll end up treating you with that Southern Hospitality because we're so happy for the opportunity. He'd say, "Nah, man. Fuck that. Yeah, we're happy for the opportunity, but they've got to pay us." Aaron kept our price high. Even if I wanted to compromise a bit, he wouldn't let me. But he wasn't being diplomatic. He was cussing people out if they didn't meet our requirements.

We ended up parting ways with Aaron because I didn't think he handled one of our deals fast enough. That was a mistake. We should have kept him. Aaron's a beast that doesn't play games and knows how to get money. He ended up representing Justin Bieber, Joss Stone, Kelis, and a bunch of other stars.

At the time, though, I felt different. Suddenly, I felt like I could do anything I put my mind to. But I needed everybody to be on the same page with me, and they weren't, including Aaron. When we did the *Most Known Unknown* album in 2005, that was the end of that era. That album's hits, "Stay Fly" and "Poppin' My Collar," were our final salvo during our prime run.

We came from Memphis, talking about robbing, killing, and tearing up clubs, and became stars doing it our way. We kept that vibe alive with Chrome. I thought we'd done a good job evolving musically and it showed when Hypnotize Minds released his *Straight To The Pros* LP October 25, 2005.

Chrome was independent and the music worked in our underground market. Overall, though, our buzz wasn't as strong as it had been during the last decade-plus. Music was changing and the label was trying to get us to go pop. I wasn't comfortable coming from Three 6 Mafia and trying to be pop stars. Moving out of Memphis was also a mistake. Three 6 Mafia was in foreign land, Los Angeles. Without knowing it, DJ Paul and I were losing our ear, our connection to the streets that enabled us to stay on top.

Then people started trying to put us with pop producers, telling us how to make songs. Columbia Records put us with a bunch of songwriters and producers, including Dr. Luke. We wanted him to make songs like ours, but the label wanted him to make music similar to what he was doing with Kelly Clarkson and Backstreet Boys.

Three 6 Mafia had never had outside songwriters before. We had done everything ourselves. We didn't know how to make things sound right if we weren't producing it. That was a foreign concept, something we'd never even considered. I wanted to win so bad though, so we tried doing what Columbia Records said they wanted. The label was trying to push us to be more like the Black Eyed Peas. Since we'd won an Oscar, Columbia was looking at us like pop stars.

What labels don't understand is that not all groups have to make pop records to go pop. A group like Three 6 Mafia just needed to keep doing what we were doing and just put a little twist on it.

I don't necessarily blame Columbia for looking at us like that. In their minds, they wanted us to keep getting bigger and bigger. We wanted that, too, so Paul and I ended up doing the pop records and it just didn't work, man. It was horrible. Dr. Luke said he liked the way I wrote, though.

We were in LA, 1,800 miles from Memphis, and there was a new wave of rappers like Gucci Mane that were coming up. The new producers' beats weren't sounding like ours. We were still making dark beats with keyboards, pianos, and strings. They were using different sounds, synthy sounds.

I used to hate that shit, but that's when the trapping movement came in like a tidal wave. Gucci Mane, T.I., and Jeezy were killing it. On top of that, we were doing shows here and there, and had some opportunities. In 2006, we did a rock song for *Jackass Number Two*, "Gettin' Fucked Up." I'd been listening to Billy Idol and Metallica and had so many rock ideas, so I'm glad we had that opportunity.

Things were happening, but then the phone stopped ringing. I was also going through a major family conflict. Project Pat had been released from prison July 28, 2005, and was readjusting to society. Upon his release, he was in a different frame of mind and didn't hit the studio right away. When he started recording again, I thought his fire was gone, that he was a little rusty.

Everybody in the camp was telling me how good his new material was, so I went to the studio to check it out, to make sure I wasn't missing something. Even though DJ Paul and I had produced everything, I thought it was terrible.

"If I was a Project Pat fan, there's no way I would listen to this," I told Pat. "This is garbage. This ain't it."

Pat wasn't hearing it. He also didn't care about the bigger picture of the business, either. Three 6 Mafia was riding high thanks to our Oscar, so Columbia Records and parent company Sony wanted us to turn in his album. Pat didn't care.

"Sony will be fine," he said.

But Sony wasn't interested in Project Pat because he had been incarcerated for almost three years.

I didn't know why Pat was acting like this. He was out of

jail, making money, and working on new music. Pat didn't want to do anything to help set up the album, either, so its release date kept getting pushed back. Project Pat's ego was so out of control that I had to ease back a bit. When *Crook By Da Book: The Fed Story* LP finally arrived in stores December 5, 2006, it didn't move major units.

Consumed by the album's failure, my arguments with Pat, and my phone not ringing, I was discouraged and worried. I was hoping to retire. I wanted to retire on my own terms, not be forced out of the game. For the first time in my career, I started to wonder if things were over.

While I was in LA and driving around, all this weird-ass music was playing on the radio. DJ Paul, Project Pat, and I, along with our homies Computer and Big Triece were doing our MTV reality show *Adventures in Hollyhood* in 2006 and 2007, and I started noticing cocaine packs all around the house we were living in for the show. I even saw some in the backyard, too. I told Pat, "Damn. That cocaine is back." Cocaine is one of the main reasons why Three 6 Mafia isn't together today. The drug usage broke the group up and really fucked up everything. Cocaine is the Devil, the Antichrist. It's a different type of monster.

I started feeling like Paul and I weren't on the same page. Paul and I had never really had an argument since we started making music together. We'd been on the same page our whole lives. But now we'd won an Oscar and we're living in LA, and then we started disagreeing a lot, having small arguments. Shit had changed.

Paul was on a rock-and-roll vibe, which I didn't like. I liked listening to rock music and I looked at the Jackass song as a one-off. That was just a song, not what I wanted Three 6 Mafia to sound like moving forward. I wanted to do old-school Three 6 Mafia music, but I was acting like I was a trap star, which was way off base. I had gone from making music the way I wanted to make it to, "Oh. This sound is hot. Let me just do it if that's what the people want to hear." Sure, it sounded good, but it wasn't Three 6 Mafia. For the first time in my career, I was *trying*. I wasn't just *doing*.

Our final Three 6 Mafia album, *Last 2 Walk*, arrived in stores June 24, 2008. It was one of our worst releases. We were in LA pretty much full-time at that point, but we should have been spending more time in Memphis. To people outside of our circle, the album showed how creative we were. But since we were living in Los Angeles, the album had a Hollywood sound. That was a mistake.

In addition to it helping me musically, I would have spent more time with my mom had I been home. When I was in Memphis, she loved going to Red Lobster and Bonefish Grill. We'd hold hands and pray. My mother would tell me that she didn't understand what I was doing in my room when I was growing up, but that she was so happy for me and proud of me.

My mom kept my Oscar for me. I didn't want anybody to touch it, knock it over, or break it, so she put it in a box in her closet. Maybe she thought having it in her house was good luck, a symbol of sorts of all that I'd accomplished. One thing I did know and that we talked about at our dinners was that we were so thankful that we made it out of the hood.

Back in Los Angeles, old problems were resurfacing. Lord Infamous hadn't been in the group for years at this point. Then a club owner I know in LA hit me up. He was telling me about Lord Infamous, that he was asking the owner for pills. I felt nervous that Lord was out in LA looking for drugs. In LA, as long as you have money the drug man is your friend. You can get whatever you want and you can get it fast.

A couple days after I talked to the club owner, Paul brought Lord to a meeting about Three 6 Mafia. Lord Infamous was so high, he was shaking and sweating. Paul wanted to play me some music Lord Infamous had done, but I told Paul that Lord was toxic to the group. I didn't want to have anything to do with that. I know that he's Paul's nephew, but the vibe wasn't there anymore.

On top of that, Paul and I started disagreeing about the music, too. He would want one song to be the single; I'd want something else. It became a rocky road. Paul and I talked and decided to put the group on hold. We'd do music together here and there, but we both got lost. For years, we both had our ears to the streets as producers. For the first time, music had slipped past us.

Pat was back in Memphis and had found all these artists. He would be at my house telling me I needed to put some mixtapes out. I told him, "I don't give away nothing for free. I sell music." He told me to go online and listen to Gucci Mane, to the new artists. He'd tell me, "Man. Y'all ain't hot. Niggas ain't playing Three 6 Mafia in the South. I live in Memphis. You live in LA. You don't know what's going on in the South."

At this point in our lives, Pat was the only person who could put me in check, just like I was the only one who could put him in check. What Pat was saying was true, but I would get mad. Pat didn't care. He was telling me the truth, that DJs would tell him that we should be putting out mixtapes. "Who are these DJs and how many records have they sold?" I'd say to Pat. "Do they have a big house like mine? Money in their bank accounts?"

And Pat was right. Lil Wayne was putting out mixtapes. It was the mixtape era, but I refused to do one at first. Then, once I saw Three 6 Mafia was really on hold, I finally relented. Both Paul and I did solo mixtapes. But I produced my whole tape, so it still had the old sound. I called it *Hustle Till I Die*.

Like I had done with *Chronicles of the Juice Man*, I included a Bible verse in the artwork for *Hustle Till I Die*. This time, I used Isaiah Chapter 51, Verse 6. *"Lift your eyes to the heavens, and look upon the earth beneath: for the heavens shall vanish away like smoke, and the earth shall wax old like a garment, and they that dwell therein shall die in like manner: but my salvation shall be for ever, and my righteousness shall not be abolished."*

Lyrically, *Hustle Till I Die* was on the same vibe I'd had since I was on my mixtape grind back in the day. Musically, it had our signature keyboards and style that people weren't really messing with at the time.

Pat's artists, though, were talking about the trap shit, streets, and drugs. I'm in Hollywood smoking weed, popping Xanax, and hanging out with Playboy bunnies at the Playboy Mansion every chance I got, but I'm on the songs talking about trapping.

I was trying to relate, but I was really out of touch. I was drunk and high on pills. My syrup and Xanax vibe had kicked in. This doctor I had would give me anything, from Actavis and Valium to Ambien. I never got anything off the street, only the real deal. Everything I had was prescribed. I didn't want my stuff cut with anything. I wanted to drink it or pop it straight out the bottle.

That's when I realized that LA is filled with professional

pill poppers. I wanted more than that, though, so I'd get pints of syrup, pounds of weed. I'd drink three bottles of the yellow syrup. I had turned to drugs and pills because I was stressed out. I didn't know which way music had gone. The dissolution of Three 6 Mafia was weighing on me and, even though I didn't know it at the time, I was homesick and disconnected from Memphis.

When I started smoking weed, I stopped writing. For some reason, my energy was so up, I felt like I could do anything, that I was unstoppable.

Smoking California weed made me realize how much stress I'd been dealing with. It's much different than what we'd smoke in the South, which is straight dirt. For whatever reason, smoking California weed made my stress melt away. It made me feel so confident. That California weed really enhanced me. I would just hit the studio, rap, and go crazy with my flow.

On top of that, California has different kinds of weed. Blue Dream was one of my favorites. I would get so high that I wouldn't think about anything. For a bit, I would feel free and would be able to spit right off the head. Sometimes, I wish that I'd been smoking like that in my early days. I'd smoke here and there, but nothing like I was doing in LA. I was smoking every day, all through the day. I was stoned the fuck out and sipping on lean. All my drug use was a temporary salve, of course. I was trying to avoid what I was going through emotionally.

I felt like shit was falling apart, but I was getting into a bunch of things, trying to make something happen. I got with a band and started managing them. I tried keeping Three 6 Mafia together. I tried acting. I even tried to model. I still had energy, and I wasn't done yet. But nothing I tried worked.

I was listening to Pat's artists. I thought I was going to retire and let Pat and our cousin King Ray run D-Brady Entertainment, a company I named after my grandmother Dee Etta Brady and launched after she passed in 2005. I also named my music publishing company DEeEtta Music after her. She was the sweetest person in the world with an amazing heart. She's the one who sent my family peanut butter and jelly sandwiches when we didn't have money to buy food.

Pat and King Ray had the artists and I'd put the money behind it, so I'd be an investor, but I'd have more of a background role. I'd work with them, be in their artists' videos, do what I could to help make them successful. At the same time, Pat had me on the internet, getting used to watching YouTube and listening to new artists.

I got tired of LA, tired of partying. I felt like I was wasting my time, like I wasn't going anywhere. I was stuck and stressed out. I had a house in Memphis, so after going to that Holmby Hills party toward the end of 2008, I spoke with John Singleton. I told him, "Man, I'm losing my mind out here in LA. The girls, the drugs, the fast life, it's too much for me. I'm moving back to Memphis."

"I knew that was gonna happen to you," John said. "You should find yourself a nice girl and settle down. You can't fuck all the chicks in LA. It's too exhausting.

John was right, so I decided to go back home. I was back in the neighborhoods I grew up in, shooting videos with all these artists. I hadn't been in the hood for five years, maybe longer. When I went to my old neighborhood and shot the "North Memphis Like Me" video, I just felt refreshed.

I had been in Hollywood, where people were so fake and phony. Now I was back in Memphis with my Memphis niggas. I felt connected. I felt loved. I understood music again. It's like I had been in a time machine. I had regained my power. The Memphis energy changed me. I was back.

I made a vow to myself. I was never going to lose touch with my city again.

Being single and having no kids, I was able to concentrate on what it really was that I wanted. The answer was simple. I wanted to get back on top of the music game. I slowed down on everything else in my life, even women. Dealing with a lot of women had become too stressful, so I had one girlfriend and just focused on my music and her.

Around this time, I also backed away from DJ Paul. I was at his house with a friend of mine. We were downstairs and I heard what I thought was luggage dropping since we were heading out of town.

My boy was like, "Was that a gunshot?"

"Nah," I told him, dismissing the idea.

Then we heard another loud bang. I was wrong. It was a *gunshot.* Two gunshots, actually.

When DJ Paul came downstairs, he was laughing. He describes what happened on "I'm Alive," which was the last song on his 2009 album, *Scale-A-Ton.*

DJ Paul and I had started Three 6 Mafia. But what we'd had was gone. I cried because I realized I didn't want to be around that anymore.

With no Three 6 Mafia or DJ Paul, I was nervous about being a solo artist. It was a foreign concept to not have a team with me. I wanted and needed to move forward, though, so I kept recording and released my *Hustle Till I Die* album via Hypnotize Minds and Select-O-Hits on June

16, 2009. I produced the entire album, which sounded like classic Three 6 Mafia. People loved my songs "You Can Get Murked" and "Ghost Dope," and "Purple Kush" with Gorilla Zoe and Project Pat. I was back on my dark, sinister vibe. *Hustle Till I Die* didn't blow up, but the feedback I got was encouraging.

Since I had money, I hired street teams, and the word was getting out in Atlanta, Mississippi, and Kentucky about what we were doing. I was traveling with the street teams, too. I was hitting the streets and I wanted people to know— to *see*—that I was still hustling. I was taking pictures with people, telling them to go put my mixtape in their car right now. I was trying to help my young artists and bring back the Three 6 Mafia buzz.

Around this time, I was passing out CDs in the parking lot of a strip club in Atlanta. Somebody asked me, "What *the fuck* are you doing out here passing out CDs?" I told them I just wanted to get that feeling back of being connected to the streets. I knew I didn't have to do it. I was straight. I could have just sat at home and stayed in my mansion. But I wanted to get back out in the streets. I wanted to feel alive again. It worked. I felt alive. I had my vibe back.

I saw how Memphis was changing. Yo Gotti was coming up. I was listening to the new artists, paying attention to how they'd talk, what they were doing, getting used to the new sound. I was pushing Pat's new artists and getting them on WorldStarHipHop. People were looking at me because they didn't know the new artists. Columbia, the major label Three 6 Mafia was on at the time, wasn't happy I was doing songs and mixtapes. They called Paul and told him to tell me to stop putting out all these songs. They weren't and hadn't been helping Three 6 Mafia or me like I wanted them to, but they weren't happy. I was out there hustling, just like we did back in the day. I didn't care what Columbia said. I was going to keep doing what I was doing.

I'd do mixtapes with Pat and we'd feature our new artists on there. But nobody was paying attention to our artists. They were looking at Project Pat and me, acting like *we* had a new mixtape out even though all these other artists' names were on there, too.

Then I remembered how I'd gone to Atlanta when I made *Hustle Till I Die* in 2009. I got in touch with Gucci Mane and he told me to fly to Atlanta. I met Nicki Minaj in the studio and had no idea who she was. She was fine, and I saw her write her rap right there. Then she started rapping, and she was dope. She didn't even have a deal yet. When she got out of the booth, I told her that her verse was crazy. She thanked me and walked out.

As fine as Nicki Minaj was, I wasn't lusting after her. I knew how to turn it on and off. I'm a business-minded person, impressed by her talent.

As all that was running through my mind, Gucci interrupted me. "Juicy, play some beats," he said. He liked one of the beats I played and wanted to use it. Then Drumma Boy comes in. He started playing beats and I'm like, *"Whoa!"* Everybody was like, "Damn." I felt embarrassed because his beats were killing my beats. I still had the Three 6 Mafia sound, which was a dope sound, but he had that new wave sound. I told Drumma, "I'm not even gonna lie. I need to get some music from you." I had never rapped over anybody's beats but mine and Paul's. But I knew I wanted to try something different.

Some people feel forced to do something different. They

think they've got to do certain things to remain relevant. I didn't. I *loved* Drumma Boy's beats and the beats from the other producers I worked with. So I got some of Drumma Boy's beats. His bass sound was louder and thicker. I loved it. Then I went and listened to some of my recent beats and they weren't hitting like that. I was using an old-school bass and technology had evolved.

Pat got some up-and-coming producers from Memphis, and I rapped over some of their beats. I no longer had an ego about it. Times were changing. I had to deal with the new producers. I knew there was a newer wave and I wanted to be part of it. Plus, I was happy that Drumma Boy, who is from Memphis, was leading the wave. My eyes and ears were now open to everything.

One thing that really helped me is that I'm a producer. I'm not afraid to say, "This doesn't sound good." I don't get offended if someone doesn't like my music. I'm listening to their feedback. Yes, I'm an artist, but I'm also a producer. I knew I could never just be stuck on myself. If I did that, I would have just been stuck in Memphis back in the day or in LA once Three 6 Mafia's buzz started dying down.

In LA after the Oscar, I wasn't tuned in to what was happening in music. In fact, I was tuned *out*. I was tuned in to *my* music. But I needed to go to Atlanta, hit the studio with Gucci Mane, smoke weed with him, hang out, and go to some strip clubs with him. That tuned me back in. I realized the Three 6 Mafia bounce was still there, but that the sounds were different.

Change was around the corner. But I had no idea what I was in for.

CHAPTER

9

SWERVIN'

THANKFULLY I KNEW I wasn't living in 1995 anymore. Because of Project Pat, I was getting on the internet more. One day on Twitter somebody told me I needed to check out this guy named Lex Luger because his beats sounded just like mine. His name was ringing because he'd made Rick Ross' "B.M.F."

I found Lex on Twitter, followed him, and started listening to some of his beats. I thought it sounded like Three 6 Mafia, but with a new vibe. Paul and I made our stuff on keyboards, so it had a more musical feel. By comparison, Lex Luger's material had a computer, synthy sound that came from people making beats on their laptops.

Lex followed me on Twitter, and we started interacting. We'd both comment on the different music we were putting out. One day, he was like, "Let's do a mixtape together." I was surprised. I didn't think he'd be interested in that. I told him I was down, though.

We linked up and he was going to do all the beats on my next mixtape. I added my little things—the "Yeah, ho!" and "Mafia!" chants—so people knew it was me, but I just felt in my heart that our music was going to do something. I told Pat I didn't know why, but I had that feeling. It was an OG mixed with a young guy, an up-and-comer that was hot as fish grease. I was finding myself and had gotten my vibe back. I was in love with music again. Lex Luger and I did *Rubba Band Business* and dropped it December 2010.

As soon as we dropped it, the tape started flying all over the internet. I was looking at my timeline and I'd never seen it jump like that. People were commenting nonstop. The crazy thing was I still hadn't met Lex Luger. We talked on the phone a lot and did *Rubba Band Business* all online. This was a whole new world for me. I used to sit with DJ Paul and the group in the studio for hours while we worked on an album.

I wanted to get that same feeling with Lex Luger, so I went to Virginia to meet with him. That's when we did *Young Nigga Movement* and *Rubba Band Business 2*. My name started getting hot again. I was feeling good, like, "Man. These mixtapes are actually working." I told Pat he was right about my needing to do mixtapes.

Around this time, I met Wiz Khalifa on Twitter. He reminded me of myself. He liked to smoke weed and chill. He wasn't a shit-starter. We vibed so well. He's one of those artists who can smoke weed and just go in the booth and spit. Other than Lil Wayne, I'd never seen anyone do that before.

Wiz is also about his business. He's very smart and reads

all of his contracts. Usually, artists don't read their contracts. They're too high. Not Wiz. He'd read every one and have detailed conversations with his manager about them.

Wiz and I developed a friendship and a business relationship. He put me on the "Black and Yellow" remix with Snoop Dogg and T-Pain. Wiz was starting Taylor Gang, so we sat down and I told him I'd help him run it, so they made me a one-third owner with Will Dzombak and Wiz. The mixtapes were *working*.

Then Columbia Records called me. They wanted me to come by the office to talk about Three 6 Mafia's new album. We'd gotten a new A&R. When I got to the office, all the interns were playing my mixtapes and I asked the A&R what he wanted to do with Three 6 Mafia. He was like, "What's up with this Juicy J movement? I think we should do the Juicy J first and then work on a Three 6 album." He said, "Listen," and opened the door to his office so we could hear the interns playing my mixtapes. I told him I'd talk to Paul. When I told Paul, he said it was cool. Although we talked, Columbia didn't get back with me. Things went silent.

I was on the road, doing shows, and realizing I could stand on my own. But just like I stepped things up musically when people were leaving Three 6 Mafia, I stepped it up on the party side of things now that I was a solo artist.

I was drinking way too much. I had gotten to the point where I was drinking Bombay Sapphire gin straight and popping pills until I would pass out. On my way back from a show, my manager Ray was taking me back to Memphis. My bodyguard Big Joe was riding with us and he put his arm around me. "Man. Please stop drinking and slow down on the pills," he whispered in my ear. "Give yourself some time. You're going way too hard."

I needed that, for someone to actually say those words to me. It made me want to get my life back in order. I knew I was living on the edge and didn't want to go too far.

The combination of alcohol and pills was making me sluggish. The double dose of depressants was slowing my heart rate down, too. I thought about what he was saying. Tears started forming in my eyes.

It hit me that I was dealing with depression. I was depressed about Three 6 Mafia. It was something that I helped create and wanted to go all the way to the top. Nobody had the same goals I had and the group was done. I was doing the solo stuff, but I never set out to be a solo artist. Yes, I had been a solo artist before I met Paul. Yes, I had the talent, the hustle, and all the ingredients to be a one-man band. None of that mattered, though. I missed Three 6 Mafia.

Paul, Lord, Boo, Crunchy, and Koop, we came up together and had a big impact on music. I was working so hard to keep the Three 6 Mafia name alive by any means necessary. I was working so hard. I had my own street team and we were working, cranking out content. It didn't matter where we were. If we were at a gas station, we'd shoot a video and post it.

I hadn't realized it until that moment, but I was mad and depressed that the group wasn't together—and that it never would or could be again. While I was making a name for myself and by myself, I was in a really bad space.

Even though I didn't know the best way to handle my sadness, I knew I didn't want to slow down. So I kept hustling and put out *Blue Dream & Lean*. Soon thereafter, I heard 2 Chainz and Drake's "No Lie." I was talking with my cameraman FIGZ! about how much I loved that beat.

He told me that he knew the song's producer, Mike WiLL Made-It. FIGZ! connected us and Mike sent me eight beats.

I didn't listen to them immediately, though. I had flown out to Washington, DC, to see my girlfriend, Regina Perera. (Now she's my wife.) I was in her bathroom and I came up with this cool hook. (I always come up with cool shit in the bathroom.) I thought that if I had the right beat, I might have something. My engineer Crazy Mike was in Las Vegas with DJ Paul. Mike is a really good engineer. Another engineer I'd had quit, and I didn't have anyone else I trusted like I trusted Mike.

Mike was going through it. He was in the midst of serious depression and had gone missing for two weeks. After calling around, I finally got in touch with Mike. He wasn't in a good space, so I put some money in his account, bought him a brand-new computer, and flew him out to DC on a one-way ticket. I told him I'd give him a job and make sure he was straight. I put Mike up at a place down the street from my girlfriend's apartment.

One night, I was standing on her porch smoking Backwoods. I talked to my boy Jay Green for a second. I went back in the room and it was my wife, Mike, and my cameraman FIGZ! FIGZ! was going in and out of sleep on the couch. My wife was watching TV, and Mike and I were in the kitchen. He set up his computer with a $100 microphone. I was smoking and had Mike pull up Mike WiLL's beat pack. I started going through the beats and I heard the "Bandz A Make Her Dance" beat.

What I liked about the Mike WiLL beat was that it was slow. It's something that's melodic, that I could hear someone singing over. It's also laid-back, and I wanted something different for this booty-shaking song. I asked Mike, "I got this booty-shaking hook, but what if I put it over this lovey-dovey, quiet storm type of beat?" He said it'd be hard.

While I was smoking and drinking a beer, I freestyled it. I started off writing my lyrics on paper, but when I started smoking crazy amounts of weed, I felt like I didn't have the time to write things down because lyrics were coming into my mind so fast. I just wanted to spit. I felt weed was like my spinach and I was Popeye. *"You say no to ratchet pussy, Juicy J can't,"* I rapped. I had Mike stop. I asked him if I should use that line. He said I should, but I wasn't sure. I tried to think of something else, but in the end I left it in.

Although I ended up with only two verses, I released it on Twitter immediately. It got hot and Lil Wayne reached out to Wiz Khalifa to get in touch with me. I talked to Wayne. He said he wanted some beats and I asked him to jump on "Bandz A Make Her Dance." He did, and I released that version, too. The song was on fire.

2 Chainz had also asked to do a verse on there. He had actually asked to get on it before Lil Wayne, but Wayne turned around his verse so quickly that 2 Chainz hit me back and asked if I still wanted his verse. Of course I did. That was my homie from back in the day when he was rapping with Playaz Circle. Then when I added both Lil Wayne's and 2 Chainz's verses, I put it out again. I made that the official version.

"Bandz A Make Her Dance" created a lot of its own momentum after I put it on the internet. I also did e-mail blasts myself, getting with a lot of DJs to keep the buzz going. I put a lot of work into making that song a hit. It didn't just happen.

Then Mike WiLL called me, told me I had the hottest song in Atlanta and that I needed to get to Atlanta *now*. I went to Atlanta, did radio interviews, and heard the song playing in every club I went to. The song was blowing up. Wiz even called me from Dubai and told me they were playing the song over there. It started charting and was getting 400 spins, or plays, a week on radio stations across the country. I did it all independently and with no major label help.

I knew I had to capitalize on this, so Regina, my girl-friend, set up a tour for me. She helped out as my tour man-ager and everything was very professional. That helped the buzz, which kept growing.

Then Columbia Records called my lawyer, Joe Carlone. They said they were calling about this guy Juicy J and that they wanted to sign me. "You fuckin' dumbasses," my law-yer told them. "You already have Juicy J under contract. Juicy J is in Three 6 Mafia."

They were like, "Oh, *really.*"

Since Columbia had me under contract, they told my lawyer that they wanted to put out "Bandz A Make Her Dance." When I told my lawyer no, Columbia said that since I was signed to them, I couldn't do a deal with anyone else, that it didn't matter what I wanted to do. If I didn't do the deal with them, Columbia said they would snatch the song off iTunes, do a cease and desist, and sue me.

I was about to make a critical decision, one I knew would make or break my career.

CHAPTER

10

LAST MAN STANDING

"BANDZ A MAKE HER DANCE" continued growing independently and Columbia Records dug its heels in. I couldn't believe how they were treating me, that they didn't believe in me as a solo artist until I made a hit on my own, that they didn't trust what I was saying despite my track record with them. I was so mad because I'd told them about The Weeknd and that I wanted to shoot a video for my song with him, "One Of Those Nights." People at Columbia hadn't heard of him and didn't want to pay the $60,000 for the video. So *I* cut the check for the $60K. Today, the video has almost 60 million views on YouTube. Nobody at Columbia could believe it. They would say things like, "You've got a good ear." I told them I wanted a position at the company where I could run it. They didn't make that happen, but I felt like they owed me a million apologies and needed to make things right.

My lawyer knew that Dr. Luke had a deal with Columbia Records and told me he'd reach out to Luke. It was a great idea because when I was living in LA, Dr. Luke reached out to me and had me write a song for Britney Spears. He never used it, but I liked him and his vibe, both him and Benny Blanco.

So Joe Carlone called Steve Barnett, then chairman of Columbia Records. "The only way we'll do this deal," Joe told Steve, "is if you bring in Dr. Luke, have him push Juicy, and be in Juicy's corner." That made sense to Columbia, and the label wanted me with a subsidiary anyway, so they put me with Dr. Luke's Kemosabe label.

Columbia Records apologized to me for all the shit they did—and didn't do—to Three 6 Mafia. They cut me a big-ass check. The money was great, but I also felt like a burden had been lifted from my back.

I was adapting to the new wave and carried the formula I used to great success on my mixtapes over to the major label system. I embraced working with different producers, and it paid off. Mike WiLL Made-It, Crazy Mike, Sonny Digital, Young Chop, Lex Luger, Dr. Luke, and Timbaland produced songs with me, something we never would have done with Three 6 Mafia or on our Hypnotize Minds label.

Through Columbia Records and Kemosabe Records, I released my major label debut solo album, *Stay Trippy*. It arrived in stores August 23, 2013, and really took off. "Bandz A Make Her Dance" went platinum. It could have gotten even bigger.

The A&R I was working with said André 3000 wanted to get on the song, too. Somehow word got out behind the scenes about André 3000 appearing on "Bandz A Make Her Dance." The news even reached Beyoncé. She told my people that it was one of her favorite songs and that she would get on it once she heard what André 3000 did with his verse.

André 3000 wrote his verse, but his team told my A&R that he felt like he didn't bring anything to the song. I begged my A&R to give me André 3000's number. André was a friend of mine and we'd worked together in 2007 on UGK's "Int'l Players Anthem (I Choose You)," which DJ Paul and I produced and on which André 3000 and his OutKast partner Big Boi rapped. But my A&R was going through someone to get to André 3000 and I couldn't track down his number either, so I never got to talk to André 3000 about getting on "Bandz A Make Her Dance."

When I lost the André 3000 appearance, the potential Beyoncé feature was gone, too. Those were big blows, but fortunately my momentum didn't suffer. My single "Bounce It" went gold. So did *Stay Trippy*. I was partying and kicking it. That's why the songs on *Stray Trippy* focus on that.

Looking back, I was relieved. I was finally able to do things based on my choices, my decisions. I was thrilled that there wouldn't be any arguments, that things were going to be smooth. I was in a good musical space. I felt like I'd brought back the classic Three 6 Mafia sound and introduced it to a new generation of artists and fans with my solo material.

It wasn't always easy being a solo artist, though. I wasn't used to rapping onstage by myself. I was doing a lot of pills, especially Xanax. I hated Vicodin, but I kept taking them. That's how gone I was on the pills.

In the back of my mind, though, I knew I was doing too much. Fortunately, I was very disciplined, so I was good at getting off drugs. I finally dropped almost everything I was doing—the Vicodin, the Percocet, the lean—pretty easily. Xanax was another story. When I stopped popping them, I started feeling muscle aches and was groggy. I didn't know what was wrong with me, so I'd pop a Xanax. When I wouldn't take it, I'd notice I felt crazy. Right then I knew I needed to get off it. I tried to go to sleep without it, but I was jittery.

That's when I told my manager Ray that I didn't feel good and couldn't sleep. I knew something was wrong, so I would give Ray my extra room key when we were on the road in case he couldn't reach me. I knew I had a problem, that I needed to get off Xanax, that I needed help because I had to take at least one pill a day to feel normal. We were in Atlanta and he took me to a doctor.

After he did his checkup, the doctor told me Xanax were easy to kick. Just start by taking half a football each day, then half of that. Gradually, my need for the pills would fade. It worked. Once I knew I had things under control, I felt a lot better about myself and my life.

Despite having done too many drugs, I was making some good decisions. Our lawyer Joe Carlone helped us clean up a lot of Three 6 Mafia's business. Back in the 1990s, our music was released through so many companies that our business wasn't as tight as it should or could have been. Three 6 Mafia was losing tons of money because of it.

People would ask me about doing another Three 6 Mafia project. At the time, I just wanted to do things myself. I didn't want to compromise. If I did Three 6 Mafia, it would have been Paul and me, and I didn't really think we were in the same mindset. I was torn because part of me wanted to do it.

But I'd often see the cocaine packs lying around our

house, which told me people were snorting. I didn't want to be around that anymore. I was burned-out on that. I wanted to make records. Paul was making EDM music, too. I wasn't. If we were going to do something, this is Academy Award–winning Three 6 Mafia. It's the *brand*. I felt like if I was going to take a chance, I might as well take a chance on my solo career. If I fuck that up, I fuck it up. When I made that decision, I felt like a burden was lifted.

For years, I had been playing so many roles: producer, rapper, executive, businessman, manager, assistant, daddy, psychiatrist, and security. Finally, I didn't have those headaches anymore. I didn't want to go backward, arguing all the time.

It worked out because my solo career kept growing. Mike WiLL Made-It put me on his song "23" with Miley Cyrus and Wiz Khalifa. Then Dr. Luke called me in the middle of 2013 and told me that Katy Perry wanted me to do a song with her. I thought he was bullshittin'. Once I realized he was serious, I was nervous as fuck. Dr. Luke sent me the song and I was on it. In less than a day, I wrote a verse and killed it. It was one of my hardest verses, bar for bar and word for word, ever. Even though I was doing a song for one of the biggest pop stars in the world, I was still myself on there. No matter who I'm collaborating with, I always want to stay in my world, my character.

I sent it to Dr. Luke. He told me that Katy Perry liked it, but that she wanted me to change the last four bars. I wrote another four bars, but she didn't like those, either. I redid it four more times. Every time I sent it to her, she'd be like, "Nah. That's not it. Just come to the studio."

Once I got to the studio, we went through each one of the four-bar sections I'd recorded. When we went back to the original one, we did a minor tweak and she said it was perfect. She said, "You're so professional. I like that. You were right on time. A lot of people in this industry, they don't care."

Before I left, Katy Perry told me she liked my chain. I told her to get a grill instead, and I hooked her up with TV Johnny, Paul Wall's business partner who became famous for the custom grills he made for everyone from LeBron James and Kanye West to T.I. and Lil Wayne. That's how Katy got her grill for the video we shot for our song together, "Dark Horse."

That song went 11 times platinum. Katy and I performed at the Hollywood Bowl and in Las Vegas at the iHeartRadio Music Festival. We headlined a show in Dubai in front of like 100,000 or 200,000 people. It was a very different world than what I grew up with doing shows with Three 6 Mafia, or even during my earlier solo career. Back in the day, we'd do a club and not know if we were getting the second half of the money. It was so shady, unreliable. Now the money was beautiful and everything was professional, straight legit. Sometimes I'd be at a festival in front of 100,000, or they'd be sponsored by McDonald's, Red Bull, Budweiser—and it was just me onstage and getting paid. Project Pat would always remind me, "This is your dream." I was finally living it.

For so long, I was hung up on all of Three 6 Mafia becoming stars. I wanted everyone to want what I wanted: the Grammys, the Oscars, money, women, and fame. I wanted to take over the world. But they didn't. They'd say, "Yeah, yeah," when I was giving one of my speeches. Then they'd be like, "Pass that joint, man. Pass the blow." They wanted women, drugs, and to get high. Lord Infamous could have definitely gotten a Grammy. He was cold. Gangsta Boo was cold. Koopsta Knicca was cold. Playa Fly was cold. They had lyrics and had the potential to be superstars.

It was hard for that mentality to make sense to me because I was nothing like that. I wanted to be the greatest at everything I'd ever done, whether I was with a group or not. Pat also told me that some people just want to smoke weed and hang out with their girlfriend. There's nothing wrong with that. That's their *choice*, Pat would tell me. I always wanted to go to the next level, though. Pat always encouraged me to follow my dream. I didn't want to stop.

I came into this game to take it all. That was my drive, my hunger. I didn't care how far I got. I was going further.

My accountants called me one day. They were like, "There are 365 days in a year. You did 340-some shows." I'd do shows and after-parties. I was not turning down any money. I was making so much money and wanted all of it. When you're in a race, you race to win. I won.

I'd call my family members like, "You want some money? How much you want? Thirty grand? Forty grand?" I would call people and give money away. I felt so blessed and had to share it. I always wanted to make sure that my family was good. Even though I'd had the problems with my father taking money, I wanted to be there for everyone in my family. And I was.

I was riding high. But a crash was right around the corner.

CHAPTER
11

WHEN GOD CALLS TIME OUT

THE OTHER FIVE THREE 6 Mafia members—DJ Paul, Lord Infamous, Gangsta Boo, Crunchy Black, and Koopsta Knicca—had been making a project as Da Mafia 6ix without me. Paul was very upset with me because I didn't appear on their album. At first, I told him I would and that I'd have Project Pat do a verse on it, too. But then I thought about it and decided not to.

It was the second half of 2013, and I was on top of the world. But I felt that no one in the Three 6 Mafia crew was happy with my success as a solo artist because I wasn't trying to get back with the group. They would do interviews or tweet shit about me. Even though they were saying those things, they knew that I was always a solid guy. They knew I like my stuff on point, on time, and that I was willing to do the legwork to be successful. They knew that I was in a different space and wasn't ready to go back to the cocaine days and all the anger, rage, and problems that came with being with them.

I knew from my incident in Atlanta with Koopsta that people coming off their coke highs can really talk crazy to you or start acting like they're He-Man. Dealing with cokeheads can make you want to kill somebody. I hated what being around it would do to me—and I wasn't even using it.

As much as I loved the group, I couldn't put myself in that position, not when things were going better than ever. I also knew that the group would fall apart without me. I was the only one trying to get rid of the drugs, but cocaine was ruining the group.

The decision to walk away really hurt, but I wasn't ready to be kicking myself again, like, "Damn, Juicy. Why did you put yourself in that position again? You know the cocaine's back."

I wanted to explain my perspective to Paul about that and a lot of other things, so I got on the phone with Ray and him. "I've always worked with Three 6 Mafia and helped out this group, regardless of what was going on," I said to Paul.

"Yeah," DJ Paul responded, "you're right. You have."

Fortunately, people were still so in love with Three 6 Mafia and what I was doing that when Da Mafia 6ix's *6ix Commandments* was released November 12, 2013, it was a major independent success. The hunger was still there. As soon as *6ix Commandments* was released, the group started making money again and doing shows, which was great. But I feel like maybe it allowed Lord Infamous to indulge in some of those destructive habits again. Lord Infamous had a real drug problem, a real serious drug problem. If you've seen the movie *Why Do Fools Fall in Love* about Frankie Lymon, it was just like that. Like Lymon, Lord was immensely talented, but he succumbed to drug use and never reached his full potential.

Lord wasn't the only one, though. While they were on Da Mafia 6ix's tour, DJ Paul told me that Boo was still using coke, too. Koopsta had already had a few aneurysms, but that didn't stop him from getting on the cocaine, either. I was shocked and hurt. Then I thought about it: the members of Three 6 Mafia had been doing drugs most of their lives. Everybody in the group was either 40 or pushing 40, but they were trying to relive their twenties.

I grew out of stuff, so I was thinking that certain members of Three 6 Mafia would, too, especially the hard drugs. Of course, kicking cocaine or heroin isn't that easy.

I was also getting other worrisome reports. One of my friends had gone to one of Da Mafia 6ix's studio sessions in Nashville. He talked about it in an interview and said that he'd never been in a room with so many members of Three 6 Mafia. He explained how he got to see the drug usage—you'd hear about it on the songs or in the streets, but he actually got to *see* it. He talked about how they really got fucked up. What you hear on our albums and on their songs, it was really real. I felt like they probably got some money in their hands and probably started turning up. I'm not judging them.

I was on a mini tour on December 20, 2013, promoting *Stay Trippy*, when one of my homies from Memphis called me. He was like, "Hey, man. My condolences."

I'm like, "Condolences? What are you talking about?"

He said, "You don't know? Lord Infamous passed away."

I just got quiet. Then I said, "For real? Let me call you back."

So I called Paul. I was like, "What's up, man? What happened to Ricky, man?" We called Lord Infamous by his first name, Ricky, when we were talking about personal stuff. I asked Paul, "Why didn't you call me and tell me?"

He said, "Well, man. I thought you were busy." I felt upset about that. I felt like he could have called me to tell me that this man had passed away.

In his last days, Lord Infamous had been using a patch to help him get off the heroin. The patch is supposed to help make opioid withdrawal easier. It still has drugs, though. From what I was told, Lord was using too many patches and he OD'd using them.

Everybody in Three 6 Mafia knows that I tried to get Lord Infamous off the drugs. I took him to rehab myself. I'd pick him up from wherever he was and tried talking to him numerous times. I talked to DJ Paul and Crunchy Black, too. Regardless of whatever other drugs Lord Infamous was doing, cocaine was always the problem.

I paid for half of Lord Infamous' funeral. It was sad. I felt sorry for him. He had had so many strokes and heart attacks. His kidneys were fucked up. I prayed for the man sometimes because it had been out of my hands. That was beyond rap, beyond business. I loved him. He was a cool dude, a real team player. If he did something stupid, he would come to you and apologize, something he'd done a lot. He'd be like, "I'm sorry, man. Juicy, I ain't gonna lie. The drugs had me gone." He'd tell the truth and that's why I'd forgive him.

As devastated as I was about Lord Infamous' death, I remained focused and kept making music. Everywhere I'd go on the road, I'd have my engineer with me and we'd set up a studio in my hotel room. Really, I'd record wherever I could. I did my part of the song "Shell Shocked" for the *Teenage Mutant Ninja Turtles* movie on my tour bus in 2014. I went in on that verse. I wasn't playing any games. I felt like this run was going to be my biggest so I was doing whatever I could to make that happen.

Great things kept happening for my crew and me. In April 2015, Wiz Khalifa put his heart into "See You Again," using the pain that everyone felt from Paul Walker passing away and putting it into the music. The song became the theme song from the *Furious 7* film and was one of the biggest tracks of the decade. The cut's video has been streamed more than 5 billion times on YouTube and it has more than 1.5 billion streams on Spotify. It's been amazing to see Wiz grow since I first heard him, before he dropped "Black and Yellow."

The run I was on was *bigger* than Three 6 Mafia. Like Wiz, I was on the *Furious 7* soundtrack. I collaborated with Kevin Gates, Future, and Sage The Gemini for the song "Payback." I was also on the hit show *Empire* in 2015. It was great seeing Terrence Howard and Taraji P. Henson on set together after working with them on *Hustle & Flow*. In the back of my mind, I wonder if *Empire* creators Lee Daniels and Danny Strong watched *Hustle & Flow* and decided to flip it into what became *Empire*. They even had *Hustle & Flow* director Craig Brewer direct 10 episodes of *Empire*.

Either way, great things kept happening. I did Rolling Loud and was onstage with The Weeknd at Coachella. All my success had put people back on the classic Three 6 Mafia sound. It was almost dead, but since I had been putting the "Yeah, ho!" and "Mafia!" chants all throughout my songs and mixtapes, people were connecting the dots. At first, Gangsta Boo didn't like that I was using that on my solo material. But when my music exploded, she was glad I was doing it because it made the Three 6 Mafia catalog go crazy.

I also learned more about myself. Although I'm back in LA now, I don't listen to the radio in LA. I don't let anyone listen to the radio when I'm in the car with them. It messes with my ears, burns them out. I was listening to mixtapes because I knew that would help me stay grounded and connected to the streets. Now that I've got my spirit back, I'm not going to lose it. My mixtape mode is where I want to be and stay.

Now I could stay in LA for the rest of my life and not lose my vibe. I'm tuned all the way in to everything. You can't put an artist in front of me that I haven't heard of. This isn't something that I have to do in order to stay on top. No. I love doing this. Now I'm picturing myself with an orchestra with violins and horn players. I've got so much creativity flowing through me.

I was feeling like I was at the peak of my powers. But it hadn't even been two years since Lord Infamous died and Three 6 Mafia was about to suffer another loss.

I was still grieving Lord, but when Koopsta Knicca died on October 9, 2015, I didn't feel the same way. To me, he was like a rat. He ran his mouth a lot. He was a nut, an idiot. Rest in peace to the man, but he didn't have a mind. He was a real crazy dude that would do *anything*. You might be out enjoying dinner with your girl and all of a sudden he pulls out a gun and starts shooting up the place.

Paul called and told me when Koopsta died. Koop had high blood pressure and I was told that he had an issue after he'd done some cocaine, which raises your blood pressure.

It was too much for his body to handle. He reportedly died from a major stroke.

I shed tears for both Lord Infamous and Koopsta. Yeah, Koopsta said a lot of foul shit about me. You can see it on YouTube. But I never wished anything bad on him. I'm the type of person that if you're going to say a lot of foul shit about me, I'm not going to walk up to you with open arms if I see you. I never found out if it was a real beef or just some shit he was saying that he didn't really mean. Looking back, I think Koop's crazy-ass attitude problems, his losing his mind, and his death were tied to his cocaine usage.

As some of my friendships were ending because of beefs or deaths, I was experiencing the most important change of my life.

CHAPTER

12

GOOD STUFF

WHEN DRAKE CALLED ME UP, I was still living in Memphis. It was back in 2010 or so and I'd known him for years at that point, before he was *international superstar Drake*. I did some songs with him before he even had a deal. Drake was calling because he was performing at the Orpheum Theatre in downtown Memphis and wanted DJ Paul and me to come through and perform a couple of songs. We did "Tear Da Club Up" and "Slob On My Nob," and killed the show. DJ Paul and I weren't doing many shows at the time, so the crowd was extra turnt. But I noticed that like 90 percent of the crowd was women. Literally. I wasn't used to that.

After the show, Drake was having some family members and friends over to this bowling alley. I went to the party with my assistant and junior engineer at the time, Teezio.

He co-wrote and mixed Chris Brown's "Go Crazy" and has been nominated for three Grammys.

But the Drake party, that's where I met my future wife, Regina Perera. I told Teezio to tell her that Juicy J wanted her number. When he explained the situation, she told him, "Why'd he send you?" So I went over to her. We talked for a while and I got her number.

I called Regina the next day. She was 23 at the time. I was 37. What I liked about her was that when we spoke on the phone, she sounded educated, very smart. She was studying to be a dental hygienist at the University of Memphis. She's very professional. Regina was fine, but her intelligence blew me away. It all really sparked me up and turned me on. It wasn't just all about her looks.

Regina was different, the type of woman I thought could have my kids and be an amazing mom. To that point, I hadn't been that serious in most of my relationships with women. I had never been in a settle-down mode. I'd been too busy partying. If I could go back, I'd apologize to every woman I'd dated because I cheated on pretty much every one of them. When I met Regina, though, I almost instantly felt like she was wife material and someone I'd want to be loyal to.

As I got to know Regina, she made me feel safe, that she would have my back, and that she would treat me right if I was sick or down on my luck. That's when the real, true love kicks in. I felt like I could trust her.

It's hard to find a great person, and even if you do, you might not like their family. But Regina's people are from Sri Lanka, and they're cool, too. I hadn't been around a woman that had all of that in a long time.

Even though we had a strong connection, we broke up

and I didn't talk to her for a few years. When we broke up, I moved back to LA and then we reconnected on Twitter. I flew her out to LA and we spent New Year's in Las Vegas with Wiz Khalifa and Amber Rose.

I realized I was getting older and had done everything I'd wanted to as a single man. In the back of my mind, I'd also thought about retiring, having a family, and chilling since about 2008, when I left Los Angeles and moved back to Memphis. Even though I'm rapping every day, it's part of my struggle, the battle over whether or not I'll be able to rap for the rest of my life.

Since Regina has become such a major part of my life, she has really made me rethink my path. I had someone I wanted to be with. I was thinking about life, not just business. Regina helped me in so many ways, personally and professionally.

My mom, though, wasn't willing to embrace Regina. I just figured my mother didn't want me to get married, like a lot of moms. When my mom would be visiting us in LA, she would cook me breakfast, but not Regina. I'd see Regina didn't have any food and would be confused.

"You didn't want anything to eat?" I'd ask Regina.

"Your mom didn't ask me if I wanted anything to eat," Regina would reply.

I was surprised and disappointed, but now it clicked. My mom was never comfortable that Regina and I had gotten back together. My mom felt that once a relationship was over, it was over. But my mom didn't understand what Regina meant to me. Maybe my mom thought Regina was just trying to get some of my money.

My mom loved Destin, Florida, so we went there as a family to hang out. My mom looked at Regina and asked,

"Why's she got shorts all up her ass? I don't know. That girl's kinda young."

I wasn't really tripping on that. That's just how my mom was, very judgmental. A lot of people raised in the church think like that, unfortunately. It's the old-school Southern way. I think she was just trying to be protective of me. My mom was from a different generation, one where women didn't wear short shorts, where there wasn't social media for people to post about their families and themselves on-line. Like I had told my mom throughout my life, "Times are changing."

But my mom couldn't adapt to my relationship. Another time, she and Regina got into a disagreement. I couldn't figure out what was happening, so I let them argue.

I heard my mom say, "I'm not the type of mom you're looking for. You're looking for somebody you can call if you and my son have a disagreement. You want a shoulder to lean on."

I didn't like it, but at least my mom kept it 100 percent real with you, no cap. That's who my mom was.

But my mom didn't give Regina a chance. My mom didn't appreciate how much she had added to my life. As she's done for years, Regina listens to all my music. She gave me a lot of great feedback on my group TGOD Mafia, the trio I formed with Wiz Khalifa and producer TM88. We dropped our *Rude Awakening* album June 3, 2016. It hit No. 3 on Billboard's Top R&B/Hip-Hop Albums chart.

We were having a great time building our relationship and got married in Las Vegas on July 5, 2016. Early in our marriage, we spent a lot of time in Vegas because I have a house there. It's viewed as a party city, but when you get into the outskirts, it's very quiet. You can get a good house on a golf course in a gated community for a great price. Being married, I wasn't trying to get sucked back into the Hollywood scene. Living in Vegas was perfect for us.

Regina is also amazing with our daughter, Kamai, who was born in 2018; and our son, Jordan Myles, who was born in 2020. As a mother, Regina really stepped her game up. She has Kamai and Jordan Myles in a variety of programs and keeps them busy.

When I got married to Regina, I wanted to be the best husband I could be. I also knew I was carrying a lot of mental and emotional baggage that I'd never really dealt with. I've been struggling with mental health issues my entire life—the "Fuck it" side and "Fear" side—so in order to get a better understanding of the type of person I am, I started seeing a therapist. I wasn't used to being married or having kids. I was used to just doing Juicy J shit. I needed to learn how to make time for everything.

Through therapy, I learned how to be more open with Regina. I was so used to keeping things inside of me. Growing up like I did, it was hard to trust anybody, but I knew I had to trust her. I got used to talking with Regina about what was going on in my mind, about things I'd gone through growing up.

Now, don't get it twisted. I still cherish my privacy. I don't really put my family stuff on social media. I don't knock anybody that does it, but I try to separate being a public figure and being a father and a husband. For me, social media is for advertising my albums, my work, my business. Social media doesn't have anything to do with my personal life.

These were all big internal changes, things I never had to consider before. Another significant change was also taking place. I used to never take breaks. Now that I'm married and we have kids, I take a lot of breaks. With my newfound sense of responsibility, I really have to take other people's wants, needs, and desires into consideration. When I think I've been in the studio too long, I make sure to go home.

Having children, it's like I've done a 180-degree turn with my career. I used to wake up, get high, make music, travel. I knew I had to slow down when my wife had our daughter. Soon after we brought Kamai home from the hospital, she woke up in the middle of the night and was crying. Regina woke me up and told me to get Kamai. That was a shock to my system. I was so used to just getting up when I felt like it, drinking whatever I wanted, and not having to think about anyone else. That was a big adjustment for me. Real life had just kicked in.

I get teary-eyed sometimes when I look at my kids. It's amazing to see somebody that you created, that looks like you, and walks like you. Seeing them smile and playing with them, those are the moments I cherish. I'm a blessed dude.

Now, before I make decisions about meetings or music, I think about them first. I'm so motivated to make sure that my kids are straight. I already have property for them, and have been putting up money for them, too. Taking Kamai and Myles to school is a highlight of my day, every day. Making sure that the kids are eating right, staying healthy, getting their checkups, and brushing their teeth is so important to me. I want to be there for my children like my parents were there for me.

At the same time, I want Kamai and Myles to have some of the things my siblings and I didn't have growing up. I want them to have a well-rounded education and to travel.

Regina and I were able to take Kamai to Sri Lanka. We threw her a birthday party there and let her see jungles, enjoy being at resorts. Next, we went to Dubai, then back to Sri Lanka and after to Hawaii. When we were in Sri Lanka and Dubai, I saw how heavy they were into religion. They were serious about their prayers, and I like that.

In Dubai, they shut the city down at around noon so everyone can go into the mosque and pray. That was very inspirational. For them, it isn't all about money and numbers. We can't just sit here and think about having Cadillacs, money, success, or even just being here. It's all about God, at the end of the day. He's the Creator who made the earth.

As I plan for Kamai's and Myles' futures, I want them to understand their background, where their parents come from. I know I still need to take them to North Memphis.

I'm also looking forward to learning more about my roots, and traveling to Egypt, Mecca, and Israel. I want to go to the places I read about in the Bible, see where Jesus walked and everything that was happening during that crucial time.

I want to pray in that area of the world, just like I do here at home. I pray for safety, and to give thanks for the health of my children. That's the vibe I'm on. We can sit here and argue with people, but what are we doing that for? It doesn't really matter. Of course, it didn't matter earlier in my life, either, but now I see a different value in things.

I get it. I'd get myself into petty situations. People had doubted me so much that once I finally achieved some success, I thought I was the shit and that my status at the top of the game would last forever. I let the Oscar go to my head. Now I see how people worship statues and plaques, those accomplishments. I did the same thing. But those things aren't reality. People are here today and dead tomorrow.

I'm working to get my life right with God. It's not an easy process. Sometimes, I feel like I'm fighting my demons and temptations every day. That's something I've been doing most of my life. I know I have to keep pushing through because God put me here for a purpose. I'm really trying to be on a positive vibe.

When people start stressing me, I don't care who they are, I'm not going to be around them. I'm not going out stressed out. I'm going out happy. I'd rather go out broke than stressed out. You have to enjoy yourself and have a clear head.

After dealing with so much bullshit throughout my life, I knew the next phase of my life was going to be the most important.

CHAPTER

13

THE HUSTLE CONTINUES

GETTING MARRIED AND BECOMING a father didn't slow me down. My career kept growing. I voiced the dog P-Diggy in the 2016 comedy film *Pup Star*. More than 20 artists sampled "Slob On My Nob." A$AP Ferg used it for his five-times-platinum song "Plain Jane" in 2017. The same year, G-Eazy used it on "No Limit," his smash single featuring Cardi B and A$AP Rocky. It went seven times platinum. The acclaimed STARZ series *P-Valley* even used "Slob On My Nob" on an episode in 2020. It got to the point where I was clearing two or three samples a day. Then, in May 2023, Derrick Milano and I produced Glo-Rilla's "Lick Or Sum" single. It's a remake of "Slob On My Nob" from a female perspective. Taking part in a female rapper from Memphis remaking one of my songs is incredible. People are loving it, too. The "Lick Or Sum" video logged more than 2 million views in a month.

Back when COVID-19 hit, I focused on making music and producing. Thankfully, I was making good money with that. It made me think that I didn't have to worry about doing shows anymore. I could just stay at home with my kids, release albums (like November 2020's *The Hustle Continues*), and make beats.

When I told A$AP Rocky I was making some beats, his response was flattering. "Are you going to make the early '90s Three 6 Mafia beats? Or the early 2000s Three 6 Mafia?" he asked. I'm proud that artists recognize our growth, that DJ Paul and I can produce so many sounds and styles. We went from sampling to working with guitar players and opera singers. I have so many musical ideas that I don't want to get locked into one thing when I'm making beats.

My lawyer told me that if a show comes along that makes sense, then I should do it. Other than that, he said I should just stay home, make beats, chill, and enjoy my kids. I've been doing that and enjoying watching them grow up.

Staying home most of the time was a new thing for me. Back in the day, I was moving too fast and never wanted kids. I was a player, and I was making too much money to settle down. But when I think about it, I don't need to be in the studio all the time. I need to be at home.

When I think about my kids, their lives are nothing like mine. It's trippy, man.

I was at the doctor's office getting a vitamin IV drip on November 17, 2021. My phone just started ringing and ringing. I was getting so many texts. Then I saw a notification on my TMZ app: rising Memphis rapper Young Dolph had been shot and killed. I was crushed. People loved Dolph. After his death, there was a dark cloud over Memphis.

When Dolph was coming up, Pat had been telling me to check him out. He was so hard and had a major buzz in Memphis. If you went in the hood clubs, they'd be playing Dolph's music back-to-back. Pat and Dolph had been talking and then Dolph hit me up in 2015 to be in one of his videos. I told Dolph I was in LA and he said, "Cool. I'll pull up out there."

Dolph came out and brought his own cameraman. I could tell he was a boss because he had his own shit. He was flying here and flying there to promote his music, and he was doing it out of his own pocket for his own label, Paper Route Empire. Dolph was fresh, too. That comes off in the video we shot with 2 Chainz and DC Young Fly, "Pulled Up."

Dolph was so impressive. His music was underground street shit, but he made it big-time and had several independent gold and platinum singles, including "Play Wit Yo' Bitch," "Major" with Key Glock, and "RNB" with Megan Thee Stallion, which I produced.

After "RNB" blew up, we had a problem. I had used a sample in there and didn't clear it. Dolph was calling me and said the group wanted money. I thought they were looking for $50,000 or something like that. Dolph told me no, that they wanted more than 10 times that. I had sampled some of this group's music years before and I'd cleared that sample with them. I don't want to disclose who they are, but we ended up working out a great deal for "RNB." It cost me $100,000. Not clearing samples can be real expensive. One day, I hope we can get in the studio and create something because I really mess with their music. That's why I keep sampling them.

Dolph and I ended up having a good laugh about "RNB."

We did several other songs together over the years, including his "By Mistake" remix with Project Pat and my song "Shopping Spree." When I was in the studio with Dolph and his protégé Key Glock, they would just spit. They never wrote anything down.

All the songs I did with Dolph and the ones I produced for him, I never charged him. He was so cool and humble. I respected what he was doing and wanted to help him.

Now I see people coming together in the city thanks in large part to what Dolph had done. A guy named Famous Animal Tv features a lot of Memphis talent on his YouTube channel. People were and are freestyling on there, getting recognition, and getting record deals.

When Three 6 Mafia was coming up, I wouldn't just jump on anybody's record. We only worked with the people we signed. That was it. Today, artists in Memphis are really working together and helping each other. That's a positive change that's happening.

Even though the big corporations aren't looking out for Memphis artists, in a way it doesn't matter. People from Memphis are hustlers. They'll work 24 hours a day just for an opportunity. The musicians, the songwriters, the rappers, they're going to find a way, just like Three 6 Mafia did, like 8Ball & MJG did, like Yo Gotti did, like Young Dolph did, like Pooh Shiesty did, like NLE Choppa did. The list goes on and on.

Maybe now that people in Memphis see the musical movement that's happening, they'll use their laptops instead of picking up a gun. I want Memphis to become a better city, so I hope these words will help speak it into existence.

As I get older, my love for Memphis continues and has only deepened. The city has so much talent. I record with young Memphis artists on a regular basis. I feel like the major labels have really overlooked my city. I still look at Memphis like a diamond in the rough. The vibes in our city are crazy. The hate is starting to fade.

Even if the music industry may not openly acknowledge it, they really love the Memphis sound. Megan Thee Stallion showed that when she had me coproduce her double platinum "Hot Girl Summer" single with Nicki Minaj in August 2019. But when I got the call to do *Verzuz* with Bone thugs-n-harmony, I wasn't interested. But I knew they were making a lot of money with *Verzuz*, so I entertained the possibility and agreed to a call with *Verzuz* owners Swizz Beatz and Timbaland.

On the phone, they explained how good being on *Verzuz* would be for our catalog. "Three 6 Mafia's catalog is already up," I told them. "Y'all don't understand. Three 6 Mafia is the wave. Do you know I'm clearing five or six samples a day sometimes?"

Timbaland was like, "Whoaaaaaa!"

The call ended and I thought about what everyone was saying, including myself.

I got on the phone with my manager Ray. "They gotta pay, man," I told Ray. "They're not going to give me crumbs."

Ray told me that Swizz had asked him, "Why were we gonna do the culture like this?"

"Do the culture?" I replied to Ray. "They sold *Verzuz* to Triller for millions of dollars. What does that have to do with the culture? They got paid, so they should be trying to help the culture get paid. I wasn't born yesterday. I've got to get a nice big check and I need some shares of Triller."

Not wanting to play myself, I then called Jeezy, who had done one of the most legendary *Verzuz* episodes, the one where he faced off with rival Gucci Mane back in November 2020.

I asked Jeezy, "I'm not trying to be in your business, and you don't have to tell me how much, but they want Three 6 Mafia to do a *Verzuz*. Is there a check there, a real bag? Would I be selling myself short if I just did it?"

"There's something there," Jeezy said. "Stand on what you've got."

After I talked to Jeezy, I felt like I had lowballed *Verzuz* with the initial amount we asked for. Ray called *Verzuz* back and said we weren't going to do it. *Verzuz* was like, "What happened?" We told them they needed to increase our compensation, that they had to make it worth it for us.

Man, they broke us the *fuck* off, so we agreed to do it. *Verzuz* treated the payout like a normal concert, so they paid us half the money before we performed. Things were looking lovely.

Before the event, everyone had a security meeting about Bizzy Bone. We were told that he was going crazy and that everyone was a little nervous about what he might do. Maybe, I thought, he was just doing it to hype the show. He was acting crazy like he always had. I didn't really care. I just thought we were all going to rock and put on a great show.

When I rolled up to the Hollywood Palladium in Los Angeles on December 2, 2021, I wanted to have a good time, throw some money into the crowd, and bring some strippers onstage. I went to the event peacefully, looking to celebrate the OG status of both Bone thugs-n-harmony and Three 6 Mafia.

Almost immediately, things got off to a rocky start. Only a few minutes into the show, Bizzy Bone felt we had disrespected him while he was performing his part on Bone's song "Buddah Lovaz."

"You ugly muthafuckas ain't finna be mocking me while I'm on muthfuckin' stage," Bizzy Bone said.

I was the closest Mafia member to him and I was heated. "Man, suck my dick," I responded. Bizzy then threw a water bottle at us and fists started swinging from both sides.

Thankfully, security swooped in and quickly got things under control. After disappearing for a few minutes, Bizzy Bone got back onstage and gave me a pound. "I'm not trying to fuck this shit up," he said to everyone in attendance. "Pardon me. Let's keep the party muthafuckin' going."

I'm just glad the situation didn't escalate further and that we kept the show going. We had so many great surprises, like Terrence Howard, 8Ball & MJG, and Duke Deuce. It was a *Hustle & Flow* thing. We had Memphis in the building.

As if that wasn't enough, Lil Wayne came out during our set, joining me to perform "Bandz A Make Her Dance." I met him when he was 14 and he's always been the same, a real one. He didn't have to come and he didn't charge us anything. No disrespect to anyone else, but Lil Wayne is the best rapper alive.

After the show, I thought Bizzy had fucked it up for everybody else and that we wouldn't get the second half of our money. We did, though.

Everybody was trying to get me to do an interview the next day, but I didn't want to feed into the negativity. I'm not a clout chaser, so I turned them all down. Also, respect to Bone for being stand-up guys and apologizing. I'm a fan of theirs, so I'm glad everything worked out.

As things were going well in Los Angeles, the situation

with my family in Memphis was dire. My mother had been suffering. She knew she had some sort of cancer, but she didn't want to know what was going on within her body. My mom just wanted to know about what to do regarding her treatments. This had been going on for months and the lack of information wasn't going to work for me. So in March 2022, I called her doctors. They told me she was suffering from ovarian cancer. The doctors were able to remove the cancer and give her chemotherapy, but then she developed liver cancer.

My mother told me that the chemo was too much, that it made her too sick, and that she was going to stop the treatment. She told me she was going to pray on it, so I had to let it be. Praying was my mom's way to prepare for what was happening to her. Some of us don't have that time to pray, to reflect. I'm glad my mom did.

I asked the doctors about my mom's prognosis. They told me she only had about five or six months to live. My mom insisted she didn't want to know anything about her medical situation, so I respected her wishes. I told my dad and I told Pat.

Thankfully my father and my sisters were with her the whole way. They were in the house with her, in the hospital with her. My dad would be there, picking my mom up, taking her to the bathroom. That's real love, being there to take care of somebody when they can't even move. That's the type of bond I want to have with Regina and our children. I want us to be with each other until the end.

Watching my mom suffer was the worst thing in the world. I felt lost, like I was in a dark space and somebody was ripping my heart out with a knife. Out of everything

I've been through in my life, it's the most painful thing I've ever experienced.

In the midst of that, I'm glad my mother got to spend some time with Kamai. They got to know each other a little bit. My mom only met Jordan Myles one time, though. He was an infant, my mother wasn't flying because of her health issues, and COVID had just started. But I'm glad she got to meet and spend time with both of my children.

My mother passed July 21, 2022. When she died in Memphis, I was in the hospital holding her in my arms. After they removed her body, I was walking out of the hospital room and I saw her shoes. That's when it really hit me: my mom isn't coming home anymore. I wasn't going to be able to say, "Momma. Make sure to get your shoes." She was gone.

Part of what made this situation so difficult was that I couldn't do anything to help my mom. I was by her side, but helpless. I didn't want to let go, though. At the funeral, I went up and hugged on the casket as they were taking her body away. I said a prayer for her and talked to her. That was it.

My mom took a lot of pain to the grave with her. She had been scarred by racism growing up and throughout her life. I don't think she ever got over her father never telling her that he loved her. Somebody in my family told me that she was still torn up that my father had betrayed her. It seemed as though at the end she still had a lot of issues about her marriage bottled up in her.

As I got to know my mom more in my adult years, it was easy to understand why she had a hard time trusting people. From what I had learned about her father and about her experiences growing up, she didn't live an easy life and she held on to a lot of bitterness.

Those feelings became more clear, to me at least, when she was sick. Toward the end of her life, I know my mom was on heavy medication, but I could tell that she was still hurting by the way that she was talking to my father. She snapped on him for something that wasn't that serious.

I know people today like to open up and talk to people about their feelings and what has happened to them. That's fine. For people like my mom, some things you just didn't talk about. You just kept them to yourself.

I miss my mom and want her to come back, even though I know she won't. That's why I left things the way they were when she was here. The Benz that I bought her was still sitting in front of her house months later.

Not being able to talk to my mom anymore is one of the toughest things I have had to deal with. She and my dad were great parents. They always made time for my brother, my sisters, and me. Being a parent myself now, I better understand how valuable that time is.

The older I get, the more efficient I try to be. I'm done trying to hold people's hands or live in the past. I don't want to go over things that happened five, 10, or 15 years ago. I have other things I want and need to do now, mainly spending time with my kids.

At this point, I really don't talk to anyone from Three 6 Mafia unless it's about business. Part of that is because Koop, Lord, and Boo have passed away, of course, but I really only talk to Paul over e-mail when it's time to do business.

It's the same thing with Crunchy Black. I see him when it's time to do the reunion stuff. He knows I tried my best to help him out, to keep him out of trouble, get him out of jail. I saw an interview on VladTV where he told the truth about our relationship. I respected that.

The last time I saw Gangsta Boo was in August 2022. I saw her at The Smokers Ball Music Festival in Lansing, Michigan, and we caught up. Soon thereafter, we spoke on the phone and she still had feelings about a time several years earlier when I'd done a show in Memphis and she got kicked out of my dressing room. I told her that was because the last time I'd heard anything come out of her mouth it was, "Fuck Juicy J. Fuck Three 6 Mafia. Fuck DJ Paul." I didn't entertain that. I hadn't responded to her because I'd moved on with my life.

I like to live my life stress free, and everything I'd been hearing from Boo was bad. So when I heard she was in my dressing room, I didn't know what she was doing there. Eventually she said she understood, especially since I hadn't talked to her in *10 years.*

I should have called her long before it got that far, but I had an ego, too. I felt like I couldn't win for losing, that people were coming out of the woodwork for me. I understand that because I'm doing my own thing and the other members aren't doing the same things that there's going to be some backlash. It happens all the time. That isn't unique to Three 6 Mafia. But I wasn't thinking about them or any of those things. I was just trying to stay out of trouble, make as much money as I could, and live a great life.

As she was talking to me, I kept thinking that she needed help. It reminded me of back in the day when she'd be high as a kite. She's a grown woman, and I let her do what she wanted to do.

I wish I would have said something. Maybe it might have made a difference. I wonder what would have happened if I'd pulled her to the side and said: "Boo. I know you're still getting high, still doing cocaine. I can see it in your eyes. I know the coke eyes. I've been around you all my life. I *know* it. You need some help. Is there any kind of way I could help you?"

I wish I could have just said that and I hate that I didn't. She could have said whatever, even if she said no. I would have been cool with that. I know you can't hold a person's hand forever, but sometimes I feel like I failed.

I remember leaving her that day thinking about how good it was to see her—but that she was *high*. Everybody was talking about how high she was.

Then, on January 1, 2023, I was hungover sitting in my theater room. I got a text from La Chat that I can't get out of my mind. "Boo dead," is what it said. That was a hell of a text. For weeks, I'd think about that text every morning when I woke up.

As I got more information about what'd happened to Boo, I felt even worse. About 10 days after she passed, I was told that the police had possession of some footage from a Ring doorbell camera. She was allegedly sitting on her porch and got sick. She made a call and was crying on the phone. She asked whoever she was talking to, "What did you give me?" She passed a little bit later. When I heard that, it was like I'd just found out that she'd passed away again.

My son was extremely sick in mid-January 2023, so I wasn't able to go to Boo's celebration of life at Railgarten in Memphis or her funeral at Brown Baptist Church right across the border in Southhaven, Mississippi. My daughter was sick, too, so I had to be at home for my kids and take care of them. I couldn't walk away from them.

I did pay for some of Boo's funeral, and sent a wreath and a video testimony. La Chat went to the funeral and Face-Timed me. I actually saw Boo's body. She looked good, as if she was just asleep. I felt like I could just say, "Wake up, Boo," and that she'd get up.

Boo and I had just seen each other a few months earlier. I feel like she isn't gone, but I know she is. Her death really made me see that life is so short and so valuable. It's so sad that everyone in Three 6 Mafia who has passed away—Koopsta Knicca, Lord Infamous, and Gangsta Boo—died from drugs. Cocaine and heroin, those are powerful drugs. Not doing cocaine has kept me alive and levelheaded.

To this day, any time I see someone post about Boo on Instagram, I cry. It saddens me because I did everything in my power to get Koop, Lord, and Boo off that coke. I was determined to get them off that shit and I failed. I made it my duty to pick people up, have conversations, get them to go to rehab, whatever needed to be done. I did all of that to the end and none of it worked. I gave my life to and put my life on the line for Three 6 Mafia. Regardless of what any of them may have said about me, they all know this. I was there from day one until the end.

Dealing with my mom's death and then Boo's death a few months later, I realized I need to enjoy every day as much as I possibly can. I'm making a point of being around people I love, whether that's my family or my friends like Wiz Khalifa, Crazy Mike, and my security. Yes, we work together, but we also just sit around and talk about life. That time is so important because we don't know all the answers. We really don't know what's out there, and maybe that's the way it's supposed to be.

I might go to the movies, take a little vacation. Sitting

back, smoking some weed: sometimes that's the best thing in the world. I went to Rick Rubin's house in Malibu, California. It's a beautiful place with a really nice studio. It's quiet, maybe too quiet, but I loved the vibe there. He looks like he's just chilling and is relaxed. He seemed very comfortable, like he has a comfortable soul. That's how I want to be. As an OG, you should live like that.

I see too many people my age stressed out. Everybody's going to get in arguments from time to time, but it's important to move past petty shit. Dwelling on things and holding on to grudges is foolish. That ain't it.

Some people love drama. I could take it back in the day, but I don't have the time or the patience for it anymore. In my search for happiness and peace, I'm letting more and more things go. I've learned to turn the other cheek and bury the hatchet with a lot of people in my life. Doing that made me a better person and kept me focused on what is important.

I've learned how to not bring the wrong people into my life anymore. If I do end up hiring the wrong person, I just fire them. I think of it like the Thanos snap. I'm not going to argue with them over the phone or in my home and raise my blood pressure. Those days are finally over. I let that stressful energy go because I know I can find somebody else. That's how I roll today.

I envision myself years from now, where I want to be, how I want to live, and where I feel comfortable. Even though I don't live there, I love Malibu and other places by the beach. I see myself as a hippie dad, living on the beach, smoking good weed, working out, eating right, praying, and watching the water roll in every morning. That's why I grew dreads. I'm getting my hair ready for the beach.

That's where I want to be one day, living with a total peace of mind, taking it easy, and not giving a fuck about the outside world. It's hard to find that, but I'm getting closer.

For now, I'm in the studio most of the time. I love creating new songs, getting calls from people like Justin Timberlake and Bella Thorne. Making music is still a challenge that I'm amped up about because I know I'm going to create something crazy. I always send people heat.

Sometimes I'll write three verses in a row and pick the best one. I don't play when it comes to music.

I'm always trying to learn, to do things differently. Right now, I'm taking piano lessons. Although I had been able to peck on the keys, I was never a trained piano player. Since I never was a Liberace type of dude, I want to get to that level, to be able to put a piano onstage and go crazy with it. I still feel like I'm growing, musically and personally, and that my music is getting better.

Today, I don't see any boundaries with my music. I used to see Prince perform on TV. He was rich, still out on the road and doing shows. I want to do that because I still have the love for it.

I want to make records about my childhood, and how drugs have destroyed lots of people. With the next phase of my career, I want to make music that is more reflective, that could help and inspire people.

After my mom passed away, I came up with the idea to make my *Mental Trillness* album. Everything that's going on in my life, I put it into this project. I reference my own mental illness. I feel like I've rapped about so much and talked about some of my personal stuff, but I've never really poured my soul into my music.

The album takes a new look at mental illness. "Bandz

A Make Her Dance" was about having a good time. The *Mental Trillness* strip club song is "Drink To Escape." It details the times where I've been in a strip club drinking and getting high just to kill the pain.

On "I'm Stressin'," I rap: *"I'm stressin'/Smoke my weed, count my blessings/Keep my Glock cocked for protection."* With all the drama I've been through in my life, I ride around in a bulletproof truck almost every day and I'm strapped at all times. You never know what could happen. Nobody's out there looking for me that I know of, but there are robbers and jealous people everywhere. I'm not extra paranoid. I just like being safe.

In this next stage of my life, I'm going to try to do things to help the community. The messages on *Mental Trillness* can do that.

Everybody should take care of their mental health. It's very important. It took me a long time to realize that. It started from some of the trauma I experienced in my home and growing up in Memphis, and went from there.

I realized I was never too open with people. For example, none of the members of Three 6 Mafia or Hypnotize Minds other than Paul ever came over to my house. They didn't even know where I lived. It's not that I didn't like them or ride for them. I just didn't trust *anybody*.

I wasn't going to do anything that could compromise my potential success. From my early days to today, I never let anybody stand in my way. If we're not on the same page? That's cool. Goodbye. I'm on the money train, and it's going to keep moving. That's why I'm still here today.

I'm exploring my creativity in other ways, too. Logic produced an entire album for me, too. It's on some boom bap shit, a sound people have never heard me on. Plus, I'm doing different types of flow on there. I'm showing people I can do it all. I don't live in the 1990s. I know I'm from the 1990s and hit it big with *Stay Trippy* in 2013, but it's all about what I'm doing now.

One of the reasons my new album is so dope is that Logic's a creative genius. Michael Jackson, Prince, Drake, and The Weeknd, these are stars. To me, Logic is that type, that level of star. He can pick up a guitar or a drum machine, or sit by a piano or whatever, and be able to make something out of it. He's extremely creative and able to work with live musicians, like DJ Paul and I would do back in the day. What he has is extremely rare. He's much more than just a rapper.

Logic and me, we're also great friends. My manager had reached out to his manager in 2015 and we started hanging out in the studio. It wasn't even about music. I'd hang out with him at his family functions, playing card games, board games, pool, and drinking Scotch. Then we cooked up a few songs after that. From there, we built a real relationship and became best friends. We're both chill, low-key, and have a lot in common. We're both married and have kids.

Recording with Logic was very different than what I was used to with Three 6 Mafia. There was no drama. I was able to just focus on having fun and making great music. I didn't have to worry about somebody wanting to have 100 people in the studio or someone else wanting to have no one in the studio, or getting Crunchy Black out of jail so he could record. Also, I didn't have to worry that one of the group members or someone else in the studio was going to pull a gun on me because they were upset. Logic and I didn't have those types of concerns, that type of friction. We were just locked into making the music as high quality as possible. This environment brought me a type of peace I'm not used to while making music.

Given my comfort with Logic and the ease with the recording process, I let him do his thing as a producer. I trust him. I'd watch him throughout the process. He'd make the music and then bring musicians in. Like me, he's a machine.

You can see people get nominated for lots of Grammys and selling lots of records, but when you go into the studio with them, you can understand why they're so successful. At the end of 2022, I was watching *The Redeem Team*, a Netflix documentary about the US Olympic men's basketball team and their quest to win a gold medal at the 2008 Beijing Olympics. In the movie, LeBron James tells the story about how he and his teammates would be coming *in* from the club at 6 a.m. as Kobe Bryant was going *to* the gym. Kobe Bryant knew that practice and preparation were required in order to reach the highest levels of success.

You can watch a game and see Kobe Bryant's greatness, but when you hear these stories, or get to be in the studio with someone like Logic, you get to see what really goes on behind the scenes to make them who they are. You understand why Kobe Bryant is Kobe Bryant and why Logic is Logic. Like them, I enjoy what I do and work hard at it. I could be home asleep or high out of my mind, but I'm still focused on being great. You have to put the work in.

More than ever, I'm into the art of making music. I want people to know all the songs on the new album, not just the singles. Those are songs for the club, but what about the rest of the art? I want people to listen to the new album like they would a new Drake, Kendrick Lamar, or J. Cole album. People consider them artists and their music matters to them. That's what I'm always striving for, too. I'm not in the business just to make money. I'm trying to make great music for the sake of making great music.

When people listen to the new album for the first time, they may be like, "What the hell?" since it's so different than the type of music they're used to from me. But when people sit down and really listen to it, they're going to say, "This man has evolved. He's still going."

Moreover, Logic and I own the album. It will be released independently, which is what a lot of the younger artists are doing today.

Making this new batch of music has helped me learn how to take better care of myself. In November 2022, I realized I needed to take a break and have some time to myself. So when I was booked to do a show in Vancouver, British Columbia, Canada, I decided to take the time to drive the 1,300 miles each way to Vancouver and then back home to Los Angeles. I just wanted to get out of my house, smoke, and vibe out, clear my head. I needed time and space away from the day-to-day grind and stress of my family to take a breather and to think. You have to give time to your wife and your kids, but if you don't give yourself some time, life will drive you crazy. I just needed some time. Thankfully, I had the freedom to be able to do something like that.

I'm also glad that I chose to drive to clear my head rather than take a bunch of drugs. It took me years to realize that drugs will help you calm down, but once the drugs wear off, the stress kicks right back in. You've got to learn how to deal with it. These days, I might take a Xanax if I have to catch a plane or if I'm really stressed out, but that's about it. I'll never be strung out on Xanax or any other drug again.

I've lost so many of my friends and collaborators to drugs. Mac Miller is one of them. We were real good friends and made several songs together, including "Lucky Ass Bitch" back in 2012. I was with him about a month before he died.

We were in the studio and he had this big box, like a party pack with a lot of Percocet and other pills. It also had some coke. He hit the coke in front of me and then offered me some. I looked at him kind of weird. I told him no, that I didn't do coke. I had heard he was on it, but I didn't know how serious it was. It was very serious.

Mac called me the next day. "Hey, man," he said, "I apologize for offering you coke. I thought you did it."

"I always told you, Wiz, and anybody else I was hanging around from your camp that I never did coke," I said to him, reminding him of our conversations over the years. "I was scared of that shit. I've seen so many people lose everything, including their lives, off that drug. I've tried the Percocet, the Xanax, sipped the syrup, and smoked the weed. That's about it."

About a month after that call, Mac Miller died. He passed September 7, 2018, from an overdose of cocaine, fentanyl, and alcohol. He was 26.

When I think about Mac, I wish I would have put a bug in his ear to get off the coke. I've seen people do some pills and smoke weed. They're still here today. Cocaine, though, that's all downhill and always a downfall. Same thing with heroin. Those kinds of drugs, there isn't any turning back.

I know that the new generations have a lot of stuff they're going to have to duck and dodge. There's so much out here to get caught up in. In the 1990s, people used to sit down and work things out. Not everything ended in a shoot-out. Not now. People don't even try to work through their differences. In fact, some people don't even work. I wonder where the parents are because some of these kids, they end up just partying. I would never let my drug use get to a point where I couldn't work, get up in the morning, or do what I wanted to do. I was close a few times, but I never went over the edge.

When you're living in La La Land—which is what I call Los Angeles—and you have a lot of success, you can pretty much paint your picture how you want it to be. You can have nannies, live where you want. Today, if I want to go somewhere, I go. If I want to buy a certain type of car, I buy it.

But I wasn't just blowing money. That's never been my thing. Throughout my career, I invested in studio time, in equipment, in traveling to give Three 6 Mafia better opportunities to succeed. I still invest in all those things for myself, but I'm also thinking of ways to flip my money and to set myself up for the future.

For instance, in 2015 Dr. Luke offered me the opportunity to join his CORE Nutrition investment team, which also included Katy Perry and Diplo. I thought the business had a lot of potential, so I invested in CORE Nutrition, which makes CORE Hydration water and CORE Organics. This proved to be one of the best business moves I made in my life. In 2018, Keurig Dr Pepper acquired CORE Hydration's parent company, CORE Nutrition, for $525 million. We all did very well thanks to that deal.

Since the water game has been good to me, I also invested in ZENWTR, the first bottled water to be plastic negative. It's vapor distilled, alkaline water and the company makes its bottles from 100 percent recycled ocean-bound plastic. They gather plastic from coastal environments and use it before it reaches and pollutes the ocean. The same people who were behind CORE Nutrition are behind ZENWTR, so I'm excited to see where it goes.

I partnered with entrepreneur Gary Vee to launch the cannabis brand Asterisk★. I also invested in video game company Epic Games, which makes *Fortnite* and Unreal Engine, among others, as well as Heliogen, an electric services company, and Instacart. I put money into the stock market and cryptocurrency, too.

Now that I have more freedom and more opportunities, my priorities have changed profoundly. When I was coming up, I had dreams of running a major record company like Stax or, later, Columbia Records. It wasn't until recently that I realized that I had achieved that goal. Hypnotize Minds ended up being like Stax, an independent label based in Memphis that put out several artists, sold millions of albums, and helped change the direction of music. Like Stax, most of our artists were from Memphis. Like Stax, we have an amazing catalog. Like Stax artist Isaac Hayes, we won an Oscar. We did what Stax did, just in a different form. Our form.

When I started, I wanted to help other artists out and be that dude. That's what I saw for myself—me sitting behind a desk at Columbia Records and running it with new ideas and artist development. I wanted to bring back the enjoyment of music, not focus on one-hit wonders. I was able to do that on my own terms working with artists I believed in from the 1990s until today.

After coming to one of my shows and seeing how kids were going crazy to my music, Robert Stringer, chairman of Sony Music Group and CEO of Sony Music Entertainment and I met. He offered me a label deal. I told him no, that I could do that on my own. What I wanted was to run

Columbia Records, hire my own staff, and run it from top to bottom. I got the sense that some people there thought that if I got what I wanted, they would lose their job. That was true. I work, so I have to be around people that work.

My Columbia Records dream didn't materialize, but the label was using my name to recruit and sign acts. People from the label were also asking me to tell artists to sign with them. "Wait a minute," I thought. "What am I getting out of this?" I felt like I was being used.

With my experience and what I know about how major labels work, I've cooled on my goal of running one of my own. I still have my labels and work with up-and-coming artists, but I'm more focused on my own kids now.

As I reflect, I understand that I've always been searching for peace. Regardless of what I had, what I was doing, what kind of car I was driving, I have always been on that quest. No matter how many women I was with or what party I went to, I was still stressed, depressed, worried, and paranoid. I'd be smiling and laughing, but inside I'd be torn up. Thankfully, I'm done with being a miserable rich person. Now being with my kids brings me peace and optimism.

Looking at my own family, I'm also optimistic that racism will subside a bit, especially in the next 20 or 30 years. More White people are dating Black people. Black people are dating Asian people. You're starting to see more and more mixed people walking around. I know racism is probably going to be around forever, but we're finally starting to grow out of the racist mentality. We're all the same. We all sleep, eat, and shit.

When I was growing up, I really thought the world would get better. I thought we'd have another Dr. King come along. That hasn't happened. Other leaders have come up and are still emerging, but the change has been small compared to what our country achieved during Dr. King's time.

Yet, in our own way, Three 6 Mafia helped make a change. We always did things that other people wouldn't do. We never gave a fuck and just did what we wanted to do, what we felt was right. Three 6 Mafia never put out a bad album. I know *Last 2 Walk* wasn't our best work, but its single "Lolli Lolli" still went platinum. We were one of the first rap groups to have a reality show. People told us not to do it, that we were selling out. Now everybody has a reality TV show.

Even with all the strife in Three 6 Mafia, we still made money, music, and even won an Oscar. Three 6 Mafia was the first and remains the only rap group to win an Academy Award for Best Original Song. We made Hypnotize Minds the biggest underground label of all time. For the 2022 NFL season, we partnered with the Tennessee Titans for a "Who Run It" promotional campaign, which used our song of the same name. We also did a Three 6 Mafia capsule collection with the Memphis Grizzlies. More than 30 years after DJ Paul and I started making mixtapes in Memphis, we're still making music and history. People are still opening doors for DJ Paul, Crunchy Black, Project Pat, La Chat, Lil Wyte, and me. Project Pat and I are as tight as ever. He's got my back and I've got his. I also have a great relationship with La Chat. We talk several times a week. I work on new music with both Pat and Chat on a regular basis.

Because we put our own money up, we own the masters and publishing for *Mystic Stylez* and all of our independent releases. Whether it's from streams or vinyl sales, I still get beautiful checks every month for stuff I did nearly 30 years ago with Select-O-Hits. They've proven to be great business partners. People are still sampling our old material, so I'm glad we made the music we wanted to make and that we did it the way we wanted to do it. It's still paying off. Literally.

That Three 6 Mafia catalog is a machine. My solo shit is legendary, but Three 6 Mafia is the blueprint. It's timeless music. That's what Three 6 Mafia has.

I'm also proud that so many of the people I worked with early on are successful today. Lex Luger, K. Michelle, MGK, Mac Miller, and The Weeknd all became stars in their own right. Teezio has worked with Chris Brown, Lil Nas X, and Polo G. I connected another one of my engineers, Shawn "Source" Jarrett, with Megan Thee Stallion right before she blew up. Source is making great money and he's happy now. Both Teezio and Source have thanked me several times and have told people how much I helped them out. Hypnotize Minds had also signed country music superstar Jelly Roll. Our protégé Lil Wyte brought Jelly Roll to us as part of Sno, a rap trio. We released Sno's *Year Round* album in 2011, but it didn't sell well, so we didn't cut a second album with them. Even though Sno didn't work out, Lil Wyte believed in Jelly Roll and encouraged him to start singing. Today, Jelly Roll is a bona fide superstar. It's great seeing all these artists I worked with be so successful.

Looking back, I've been a superstar most of my life. Three 6 Mafia started underground and weren't the biggest group in the world, but we had money, houses, and real estate at a young age. We did what I wanted us to do. We opened the door and kicked that muthafucka in. While I was living it, though, I didn't think I really made it until we won the Oscar. That's when I felt like everybody knew who we were. Thanks to what we did, Memphis is going to keep going, and people know who opened that door.

Music has had a lot of great artists who have left us far too soon, from Marvin Gaye and Michael Jackson to Prince and Rick James. Those artists left a stamp on music that you can still hear today. Three 6 Mafia has, too. So many people's music today sounds like Three 6 Mafia and Project Pat. It's normal for someone to say, "Oh. That sounds like Three 6 Mafia." That's because so many artists are sampling the *shit* out of our music—everyone from Drake and Cardi B to A$AP Ferg and Freddie Gibbs, from Travis Scott to $uicideboy$.

When you think about rap and who has made a big impact on the genre in the South, you've got to say Three 6 Mafia. You've got to say Project Pat. Of course, there are others like OutKast, Uncle Luke, Master P, Cash Money, and Lil Wayne, but we're on the list. We are the Princes and the Michael Jacksons of our era. It's a blessing to have had that kind of impact.

I always knew Three 6 Mafia was special. I just didn't know it would be what it is today, still enjoyed by millions of people and being sampled by dozens of artists. Back in the day, I would often tell Paul, "We built this shit, and we're going to finish this shit on top." We're still making great music and doing big shows, too. I think it's going to keep getting bigger and bigger.

As I keep going, I'm not repeating myself. I'm a real artist. I can make any type of music, jump on a song with Katy Perry, collaborate with GloRilla, do something with Diplo, make an album with Logic, executive produce a Ty Dolla $ign album, or work on a hook with K Carbon. I want to branch out to scoring movies and television. Alexandre Desplat, who composed the music for Guillermo del Toro's *Pinocchio*, is somebody I'd love to collaborate with. John Carpenter, who did the music for the *Halloween* movies, is another one. It'd be something different, something new. I know my sounds and style could bring something to the table.

I give all my glory to God. I'm thankful for everything I have, and I don't ever want to give up. I don't ever want to stop making music or give up on my family. I want to keep going. I feel like there's more to do. I've proven myself over and over again. As long as I keep on making music and doing creative projects, I'm going to prove myself again and again.

★ ★ ★ ★ ★

ACKNOWLEDGMENTS

SOREN BAKER
ACKNOWLEDGMENTS

Juicy J, DaVida Smith-Baker, Loren Baker, Alberta Baker, Stanley Baker, Grant Baker, Dion Baker, Ray "King Ray" Brady Jr., Jorge Hinojosa, Robert Guinsler, Peter Joseph, Three 6 Mafia, DJ Paul, Lord Infamous, Gangsta Boo, Crunchy Black, Koopsta Knicca, Project Pat, Hypnotize Minds, Jordan Houston Jr., Grace Heck, Allen Gordon, Tresa Sanders, Tony Ferguson, Liz Hausle, Yvette Noel-Schure, Andre Morris, Eden Railsback, Emer Flounders, Lee Tipton, and Taryn Ortolan.